"When I met Drew ᴰ  ing
RockStar. He is one of ᴺe.
Drew understands this ; a
pulse on where the pro. to
Make a Fortune in Network Marketing" will help a lot of people achieve
success. Well done Drew!"

Craig Duswalt, CEO RockStar Marketing

"I believe that Drew Berman understands the demand on business
people, to build strong relationships with networks of people in order
to create powerful masterminds that brand him as a leader, and an asset
to anyone looking for answers to success. You will gain valuable wisdom
from Drew. Take his advice and put it into action and you too will see
massive results."

Jerry Myers, President and CEO, Freedom Now

"Drew Berman's book is unbelievable! In just a few pages he really
captures the essence of the industry, the essence of what it takes to succeed.
Really listen to what he has to say! Just listen to him."

David Wood, Chief Training Officer, Isagenix International

"Drew is one of the few people to successfully blend the online world
with the offline world of Network Marketing, which is key to unlocking
great wealth and freedom as a network marketer. A great connector,
marketer, and leader, Drew will help you reach your goals and show you
how the top 1% make their fortunes."

Brian Fanale, Founder and Owner My Lead System Pro

"This is a must read guide for anyone who's thinking about starting or has been struggling with Network Marketing. It's practical and straight forward. It's full of insight and wisdom. In fact, a lot of Drew's insights are applicable to people who own or run traditional businesses. I've watched a lot of people start and fail at Network Marketing. This book could prevent a lot of failures and seed many successes"

Lisa Hayes

"Worth the investment of time and money...so that you can begin to make your fortune. It's no fluff, direct, useful, and you can read it in just a few hours of dedicated time and walk away satisfied that you invested in the book, your time and now have action steps to take"

Rick Clemons, Keynote Speaker,
Bold Move Expert, Status Quo Disruptor

Berman's book is a no-nonsense guide to accelerated success in Network Marketing from a man who does what he writes about and makes mega-bucks because of it!

Louis DiBianco Professional Actor, Podcast Expert,
Author, Professional Network Marketer

Drew Berman's "How to Make a Fortune in Network Marketing" has the perfect mix of information and simplicity. It truly is a great primer for people who want to get started in Network Marketing, or for those who want to improve their skills and take it to another level.

It's a short read, without any fluff. Drew literally takes you step by step, so that in a short time, you will have all the information you need to succeed.

Joe Crescenzi, Professional Blogger,
Network Marketer, Entrepreneur

"A leader has vision, great communication skills, honesty, integrity, humility, and a great sense of humor. Seek and you shall find. Leaders come forward when the need is greatest. A leader makes decisions and takes action and that is what it takes to attain goals. Fortunately, I have found such a leader in Drew Berman. "

Seth Lefferts, Musician professional Network Marketer

"Drew Berman has mentored countless entrepreneurs, teaching them the skills and habits required to achieve their dreams through free enterprise. His success has been attained through leading by example - you deserve to follow Drew!"

Erica Combs, Business Coach

"I just wanted to say thank you for who you are! As a trainer myself I teach, train and inspire thousands of people around the world and I will tell you - YOU INSPIRE ME! To inspire means to awaken someone's spirit! You did that for me tonight and before on other occasions. THANK YOU!"

Mitja Kadow

"There are some people that are born leaders...and heed their calling. Drew Berman is living his purpose, with great passion and dedication to those lucky enough to be partnered with him. His positive attitude is contagious, and you will marvel at his witty and intelligent mind! I was inspired by Drew, from the first moment I met him and I feel privileged to call him my friend."

Ellen Bradley Ganus, Professional Actress,
7 figure Network Marketing Professional

"Drew Berman is one of those individuals who is a true gift to the industry of Network Marketing. His passion, his integrity, his commitment to grow, his vision of what is possible, epitomize what makes our industry great! Network Marketing is a new paradigm of how business is done and how massive success is achieved. Drew Berman has been and continues to be a huge contributor to this very positive shift in our Network Marketing industry."

Ron Reid, Network Marketing Million Dollar Earner

"I have been working with Drew Berman personally for the last couple of months and it has been a privilege to have coached him, partner with him in business, as well as watch him grow and become the great leader and producer that he is. If you are seeking to learn from someone that just plain knows how to produce and get things done, then you definitely deserve to connect with Drew Berman and learn how to do what he did to get the results that has achieved."

JD Buckridge, The Branding Specialist

"Drew Berman is a leader of top home business entrepreneurs who exudes boundless energy and magical passion for turning dreams into reality. His creative approach and attitude of success is attractive and empowering. He instills confidence through an engaging style and intelligent expectation that produces results. If you have an opportunity to work with and learn from Drew Berman, DO IT!!!"

David Schafer, Internet Guru

"Drew has come through for me, backing up his enthusiasm and passion for what he does, with practical coaching tips he hands down to his team. There is an alignment of Drew's actions with his purpose and passion that makes him stand out as a team leader. There is a sincerity and honesty that one experiences. Another crucial factor is that Drew makes himself available. When you need the advice he can offer from his experience, Drew is always there for you. You won't be waiting for a call from someone who makes you feel he's too busy for you. You'll get a call from a committed mentor and partner."

Dr. Henry Sobo

YOU CAN HAVE IT ALL

─────────

Welcome to YouPart2. You've gotten this far. Pat yourself on the back. Know that the best is yet to come.

You are here because you want more out of life. You are either sick and tired of being sick and tired, already successful and want more, or somewhere in between.

Perhaps you are looking to go from good to great, looking for an exit strategy, or looking to make mega bucks. Maybe you want to make the world a better place and have fun doing it. This book is all about you, and assisting you on your journey.

There is a way to have a lifestyle by design, and you have probably heard of our business model. Some call it referral marketing. Others call it relationship marketing. Most know it as Network Marketing.

In the gig economy, where many have a side hustle, most know that Network Marketing has become a hip, savvy business that is attracting successful people from all over the world, from many professions. Some, still think it's a curse word - and that's ok.

In the pages that follow we will show you the truth of this business, and clear up some myths.

Let's begin this journey.

You Can Have It All.

FREE GIFT!!

Before going any further I want you to have a free gift. Go to www.drewberman.com and get your free training on prospecting and recruiting.

It's the exact system I used to enroll

» A professional actor from another country and help him create a residual income for over a decade

» A woman who had been in over a dozen companies, found me online, then hired me to be her coach

» A 7 figure earner, Network Marketing Professional, no longer in love with his company, looking for his next chapter. This man was a Networker in transition

» A successful entrepreneur who was looking for a way out of his successful business so he can have more free time, and

» A young nurse who wanted more then anything a side income that would replace just one nursing shift so she can spend more time with her daughters.

Once you get this training, you will start attracting people to you and you will be able to prospect and recruit on demand. Instead of chasing away prospects, you will have more people wanting to join. As an added bonus, you will get a one time offer for a $97 course on closing, follow up and team building - for only 7 bucks. That's right. Invest 7 dollars into one of my most popular courses and learn the exact system I used to build a legacy team in over a dozen countries. If you are not blown away by the training, I will refund your $7. That's my ironclad money back guarantee.

So head on over to www.drewberman.com get your free gift.

This journey is going to be fun and profitable.

Now, let's get started.

"What sets Drew apart from all the others is his willingness to Take Action. This single trait is responsible for all the wealth in Network Marketing. Drew will teach you how to overcome your fears & limiting beliefs so you can Take Action consistently and create massive success."

Evan Money, Ph.d, #1 Bestselling Author,
Life to the Full Expert

FOREWORD

———

I have had the honor of coaching and mentoring Drew Berman over the past 10 years. He has been a dedicated student, entrepreneur, coach, and speaker.

His level of commitment and perseverance to personal development, self-improvement, and mastering the skills, habits, and mindset of an entrepreneur have led him to grow and achieve new levels of success personally and professionally.

Drew had gone through the trials and tribulations to achieve success. I am honored to endorse this book as a must read if you are serious about the Network Marketing industry.

Jeffery Combs, President of Golden Mastermind Seminars, Inc.
www.GoldenMastermind.com

YOU CAN HAVE IT ALL

IT ALL

The Ultimate Guide to Having Fun,
Making Money and Living the Good Life

Drew Berman

Motivational PRESS®
LEADERS IN GLOBAL PUBLISHING

Published by Motivational Press, Inc.
1777 Aurora Road
Melbourne, Florida, 32935
www.MotivationalPress.com

Manufactured in the United States of America.

ISBN: 978-1-62865-656-5

Warning – Disclaimer

CONTENTS

For Corey, Tyler and Noah; my love and inspiration

For all entrepreneurs, seasoned professionals
or those of you just starting on your new journey.

BEFORE YOU READ THE BOOK
- READ THIS!!!

Hi. My name is Drew. I'm from New York but I currently live at DrewBerman.com. I teach network marketers how to go from hobby income to professional income. If you're ever wondering where to get proper Network Marketing training that can help you double your business in half the time, you found your new home.

Before going any further, I have a free gift for you. Go to www. drewberman.com for your free training on prospecting and recruiting. This is the exact system I used to personally enroll over 700 people and grow a team to over 15,000. It took me 25 plus years with a marketing degree, 20 plus years in business, 17 plus years in Network Marketing, 12 plus years with the same company, tens of thousands of dollars in personal development and thousands of hours studying this to come up with the exact system to help you win and win big. And you can have it for free. Go get it at www.drewberman.com. While you are there, you will see some other goodies as well.

Ok now that we got that done, let's get to work. I am super excited to get to know you and hear your story. Then together we can create your story Part 2. Together we will get you from where you are to where you want to go.

I have 3 strategies for you that'll help you on your journey.

I've been a Network Marketing professional since 2001 helping networkers like you go from good to great.

Strategy number 1 is go professional. Become a professional. Think about what other professionals go through in their life and in their business and on their journey to become top income earners. Whether it's becoming a teacher or a dentist or an athlete or a Broadway actor or even an engineer, you have to go through some training. You have to adapt the fact that you're going to be one of the best. Because of the law of immersion, you're going to immerse yourself into a career.

If you wanted to learn Italian right now, you'd have to start from scratch. You'd have to maybe get an Italian coach. You might have to get a book on Italian. You might have to go to Italy. You might have to take some Italian courses. You might have to study after hours, so that is strategy number 1, go professional, treat this like a career. Yes, you can make a lot of money quickly, but what's more important is you can make a lot of money over the long term. Yes, it's a 2 to 5 year plan, but I like to teach it's a 10 to 20 year plan. You want to become a professional. Be a stand for your profession. That's strategy number 1.

Strategy number 2, when you're out prospecting and recruiting for your Network Marketing company, I made one shift a long time ago that got me from a 4 figure monthly income to a 5 figure monthly income. Here's the shift. Instead of promising big amounts of money, because it is possible to create large amounts of money in Network Marketing; that's why I chose this profession. It's a leveraged profession. It's a business where you can work smarter not harder. It's a business where you can have international reach. It's a business where you can learn the skills and grow.

Yes, you can turn it into 6 figures a year. You can turn it into 7 figures a year, but what's more probable … see, we go from possible to probable … what's more probable is, "hey, are you open to some extra ways to make some money. Are you open to some extra weekly cash flow? Would an extra $1,000 or $2,000 a month help you in this economy? Based on everything that you have going on, if we can show you a way to increase your income by 10 or 20%, that would help, wouldn't it?"

See, when you start talking in percentages, people understand. If you're talking to someone who's making 50 grand, and you're talking to someone who's making 500 grand, and you talk about making an extra 5 or 10 grand, you're going to be having 2 very different conversations. If you say to most professionals you can show them how to make an extra 10% to their income, keep the expectations realistic. Talk about making an extra couple hundred a month or a couple thousand a month, that shift for me ended up making me a lot more money than promising people big money on the front end. That's strategy number 2.

Strategy number 3 is ... In this book, I talk about the gradient. Now, the joke I talk about the gradient is if you met someone at a restaurant or a bar and you said, "Oh, hey, I really like you. Maybe we should go home, maybe get married, have 5 or 6 kids, buy a house, travel around the world,be married forever til death do us part," that might be a little awkward when meeting somebody, right?

You want go out on a date. You want to see if there's chemistry, if you have some things in common, if you have some of the same views, same goals, you might want to go on a 2nd date. You might want to do a little ... kissy-poo. Then you can go through the gradient of spending the rest of your life together and having kids. I write about that in this book. What's easier to walk on, a gently sloping ground or a steep hill? See, a lot of people in networking marketing are so excited because we offer a better life and a better lifestyle. They're so excited that they go into the marketplace and that excitement comes off weird.

If the gradient is too steep, people won't want to come play with you. You want to use the same principle of gradient in presenting your opportunity and building your business. You don't just want to say to me, "Hey, if you join right now, we have a super juicy juice company with products from the Himalayas and you're going to live forever and they're doctor-approved and if you sign up now, we can put you on auto ship and then you can fly out to the company convention and we have millionaire upline that are making lots of money and they can help you." You lose people. Keep it real, keep it normal, don't make it weird, and you're going to have great success.

These 3 steps that'll help you double your income and double your time off, double your money in half the time. One, be a professional. Dress professional, act professional, read books about the profession. Two, don't promise vast sums of money. Third principle, the gradient. When we meet someone, we want to get to know them in relationships as well as in business. The gradient in networking marketing, offer it slow, allow them time to earn and time to learn. We have a learn and earn program, that's the gradient.

Now, for more marketing tips like this, go to DrewBerman.com. In fact, do that now, enter in your contact info, and we'll send you a free gift on 7 secrets to prospecting and recruiting. Make sure to subscribe to the YouTube channel. We help network marketers go from hobby income to professional income, and you deserve the best. Thanks for stopping by. I am so glad you have this book. I believe the principles will help you no matter where you are on your Network Marketing journey. Just getting started? No worries. We got your back. Been around a long time? Awesome sauce, lets rock. Love your company but feeling stuck? Don't worry, be happy - we got you covered. Confused and not sure what to make of Network Marketing - hakuna matata… welcome home. We got this!

MY ROOTS

Fresh Meadows, Queens NY

Stuyvesant HS

Peg Legs Football

George Washington University

Pi Kappa Alpha Fraternity

Royal Prestige

Landmark Forum

Peak Potentials

Odyssey 2000

Manhattan Apartments

Quixtar

World Wide Group

Isagenix International

Millionaire Mind Intensive

Enlightened Warrior Training Camp (AHO)

Wizard Training Camp (So Be It)

World's Greatest Marketing Seminar

MyLeadSystemPro (MLSP)

Magnetic Sponsoring

Ridgefield CT

RankMakers

GoPro

Chamber of Commerce

Maverick Millionaire

Extreme Focus International

Ceo Space International

BONUS CHAPTER

Hello.

Perhaps this is our first time meeting, or maybe we've crossed paths before. Maybe you found this book online, you bought it in a store, you won it, or some one gifted it to you. Did we meet at an event? Did it come as a bonus in one of our training courses? Either way. I'm glad you are here. You are either just getting started in Network Marketing, you've been around for awhile, or you are a seasoned pro. This profession is finicky and I hope to short cut your success. I've been doing this a long time and have had many failures, and many successes. I've laughed, I've cried, and I've made many many lifelong friends. Network Marketing for some is still round peg square hole, and for others it's the best business imaginable

There are 3 types of people. Some think Network Marketing is the greatest business model on the planet. They love passive and residual income. They love the concept of leverage. They think it could be a great plan B and some even think it can be their plan A. Then there are some people who think this is the devil's work. They had an aunt many years ago who had a garage full of shampoo. They have a friend of a friend who lost a lot of money in some bad deal. And then there is a group of people that heard of Network Marketing, they have seen some folks have success, but they don't really understand what it's all about.

So we are going to go through all that together. If at any time you are confused or lost, just reach out to me at dbi@drewberman.com. Either me or one of my teammates will get back to you. We can help you navigate through these waters, so that you can impact more people, have more fun, and make more money.

Make sure to visit www.drewberman.com often. There you can not only get your free training on prospecting and recruiting, you will also learn some of the exact systems I used to personally enroll nearly 700 people and grow an organization to over 15,000. Was it easy? No. Did I work hard? Yes. Go grab the training - it will show you the specific strategy and language I used to personally enroll

- » A grandma on the street corner in NYC- how we got her involved, and on autoship for over a decade

- » A fitness instructor on a Cruise - and how we helped her and her family pay her monthly mortgage for 11 years.

- » a successful network marketer that had a falling out with her previous company and how she has become an integral part of our team

- » and how I personally enrolled a massage therapist, from a business card I picked up at a doctors office

And a lot more. So before you do anything, go to www.drewberman. com and get some gifts and free training. Plus you'll see some cool stuff that will help you on your journey

Let's get to know each other. I look forward to being your friend, guide and mentor as together we learn how to Make A Fortune in Network Marketing.

The truth is most people who graduate college never read a book after school. Most people who get their real estate license never sell a home. Most people who get involved in Network Marketing never make any money. In fact most people in Network Marketing never even sponsor one person or find one customer. And sadly, most people who buy a book don't read beyond the first chapter.

But not you! You want more out of life. You want deeper relationships and more fun. You want to make money so you can have the good life. You want to contribute more … in fact those successful in Network Marketing are more concerned with contribution then they are with accumulation. You are different. You chose Network Marketing because you want more out of life, and you chose this book to win in Network Marketing, and win big.

And your timing is perfect. Wherever you are in life, Network Marketing can be the catalyst to help you go from good to great. Whether you need help finding the right company, or learning the habits, mindset, and skills to make more money and have more impact in your current company - I can help. Perhaps you are brand new - putting your pinky toe in the Network Marketing ocean. Maybe you have been around for a while but have not yet had success. It's possible you have been in one or more companies and have not yet found your home. And maybe, just maybe, you are experiencing a great deal of success and wanting more. More money, more impact, more fun, more duplication. Most people are attracted because they want more money or more stuff. Some are attracted because they want to have more freedom, more impact, and more fun. I have seen more success with people who focus on impact than on income. It's okay if you want to make more money. And it's ok if you want to make a lot of money. It's even ok if you want to make GANGSTAH MONEY. Just focus on helping more people.

Some are referring to this as the gig economy. Everyone has a side hustle. Whether you are single or married, DINKS (double income no kids) or in a large family… when done right you CAN make a fortune in Network Marketing, and I will be your loyal guide. I'll teach you how to be the trusted consultant, rather then the slippery salesman. I'll show you what to say and more importantly what not to say. For instance say "are you at all open to an additional stream of income if it does not interfere with what you are currently doing. Don't say "are you interested in a business opportunity" . Say "if you could improve your life in any way this year, what would you do better or different?" Don't spend 45 minutes explaining why someone should buy your product or join your company if they haven't expressed interest.

Let's put some things into perspective. No matter when you are reading this there is going to be an Olympics coming up, summer or winter, in about 2 years. In about 2 years dozens of athletes will be on the podium, winning a medal for their country. Hundreds of athletes will compete. Thousands will be involved from trainers to staff to organizers. Tens of thousands will see the games live. Hundreds of thousands will be impacted in the local country. Millions around the world are going to watch on TV.

In 2 years, dozens and dozens and dozens of people will make tens of millions of dollars in Network Marketing, maybe even in your company. Hundreds, if not thousands, will make millions. Hundreds of thousands will create 6 figure incomes. Millions are going to make an extra $2,000-$5,000 a month. You get to choose what game you want to play. You get to choose what level you want to participate.

Network Marketing is set up so that someone who has heart, desire and discipline can make a fortune in Network Marketing. You need the right company, the right timing, the right team and the right mentor. I can be your mentor, your guide, through this incredible journey of Network Marketing. Get some duct tape, we gonna knock your socks off.

PREFACE

———

The story is told of a millionaire in our profession who went to an appointment with his accountant. After reviewing the millionaire's income and profit/loss statements, the accountant was astonished.

"I need to know what business you're in," the accountant stated, desperation filling his voice. "You make more in one month than I make in a year! What is your business?"

The millionaire began to talk about the product and about the business, but the accountant stopped him in mid-thought.

"Oh yeah," he said airily. "I've been to one of those meetings before."

The millionaire was surprised. "Really? So you already know a little bit about what we do, then. What did you think?"

"Oh, I didn't believe a word of it," the accountant said, laughing. The millionaire looked the accountant and stated simply, "I did."

We associate success with wealth. We also want to be healthy enough to enjoy the fruits of our successes.

Do you remember hearing this familiar rhyme? "Early to bed, and early to rise,

Makes a man healthy, wealthy, and wise."

As well-known and oft-repeated as it may be, this pithy proverb points to the three great desires of mankind in the 21st century: The desire for wealth, the desire for health (physical, spiritual, and emotional), and the desire to be (or at least to appear) intelligent. The order of these priorities may change based on personality, but all three boil down to one simple concept that everyone talks about but relatively few achieve: Success!

Becoming successful in any profession requires an immovable belief in three things: the product, the process, and the presentation. I assume that you, the reader, have thoroughly researched your product and that recognized professionals in your field endorse it, and that they have done so with honesty and integrity.

Because of the current economic downturn, Network Marketing as a process really needs no defense, for it too has been studied at length by many of the more recognizable professionals in the field and has stood up to the tests of integrity and replication.

As you begin your journey, beware: Network Marketing can be a VERY expensive hobby, or it can be a VERY lucrative business.

Robert Kioysaki (Rich Dad/Poor Dad), Donald Trump, T. Harv Eker (Secrets of the Millionaire Mind), Paul Zane Pilzer (God Wants You to Be Rich, The Next Millionaires), Bob Proctor (The Secret), and many other wealth and finance experts endorse this profession.

Even for those who believe they are "in a recession" there is indeed a way to RECESSION PROOF THEIR LIVES. In fact, next time someone even mentions the word "recession," how about saying this:

"What if I can show you a way to opt out of the recession?"

While some people are suffering during this economy, others are thriving. Which class do you want to enroll in? I took that concept from Jim Rohn, one of the greatest business philosophers of all time. While the news is trying to convince you of a hurting economy, you can take control of your OWN economy.

Here is another one of my favorite "pick up lines" for prospective business partners:

"You know how people complain about the recession?" (Pause)

"We help them create an extra income stream to offset the current economy."

The ability to use this language with integrity and confidence is one of the many reasons that Network Marketing has grown and evolved over the last 10 years into a very sophisticated and lucrative business. And yet it is simple for someone to start, and earn while they learn. Best of all, you don't have to leave your current job or career to get started.

If your goal is to create an exit strategy, have an additional stream of income, get out of debt, fire your boss, or get rich, then Network Marketing may be for you. Why not?

It is a profession with: No boss, No employees,

No long commutes, No traffic jams, No cost entry barrier,

No educational requirements, Little to no overhead expenses, Little to no risk,

No limits to growth, No begging for raises, No need for real estate capital,

No barriers based on race or gender, Huge tax advantages, No shipping, No inventory,

Little to no customer service, No product development,

A supportive team that you choose and that chooses you, teammates who share commons goals and dreams, I could keep going...but you get the picture!

There are several pathways to help you achieve your goals within the profession that have received amazing results. Many of these tools will be expressed in the pages of this book; however, as with other tools, they only work if they are taken out of the box and used.

This brings us to presentation, which largely depends on you, the reader, and your commitment to your goals. I can open your understanding to many of the teachings I have spent countless hours reading about, learning, mastering, and promoting, along with many of the tools that top-level executives created and used, but commitment must come from you.

Come to think of it, at this moment the only thing standing between you and your dreams is…you.

My 30-second story is proof of that. Although we will discuss the power of the 30-second story in an upcoming chapter, allow me to share it with you now:

"In February 2006, I was in the advertising business when a friend came into the office and mentioned that he had lost 40 pounds by using a nutritional product he had heard about. I was never interested in weight loss as a product or as a business, but I was intrigued by the concept of nutritional cleansing. After I tried the cleansing program, my chiropractor noticed that I was adjusting much more easily than usual. When I told him about this cleanse product, he did the same program and lost 12 pounds. My father went on the program and lost 56 pounds, and as a result, became healthier, leaner and had a lot more energy. Because of this, he developed a healthier lifestyle and he no longer struggles with the blood sugar issues he was facing before.

So then I went to work. I started telling people the story. Ten hours a week part time on the side I was helping people get healthy. Within ten months I replaced my working income, and within the next ten months

I turned my monthly income into my weekly income. My wife, Corey, was able to leave her full- time job in corporate real estate. We love the journey to health, wellness, and financial freedom we are experiencing."

See what I mean? None of this would be possible except for my belief in the product, process, and presentation. The book you are now reading is a compilation of my own personal study and the concepts and applications I have spoken about in conference calls with associates and executives around the country. I have had the ability to train with elite athletes, millionaires, doctors, stay at home moms, and people like you and me that just want more out of life.

David Wood, a successful executive coach and trainer and one of my personal mentors, has stated, "students mentor students." I became successful in this business because I became a student of it, and I encourage you to study the field of Network Marketing in depth for yourself. In other words, we are all students, and we all help each other. We are all learning, but we have a great "learn-while-you-earn" program, or even better, an "earn-while-you-learn" program!

One could write entire books about each of the many nuggets of wisdom in this book (and again, I have already read many of them). As you read on, I would suggest that you do two things. First, envision your own definition of "success," whatever it means to you. Success means different things to different people, and it is only your definition that will motivate you. Secondly, I encourage you to make notes for yourself about the tools and processes that you want to study in greater detail. The only avenue for positive change in the profession and in life is personal growth. If you will fulfill these two requests, your potential is limited only by your imagination. I believe in you, more than you will ever know.

To your success! Drew Berman

www.DrewBerman.com

CHAPTER 1

LIVING THE LAPTOP LIFESTYLE

Laptops and smartphones. Layoffs and downsizing. Telecommuting and working from home.

These are not just words and not just tongue and cheek expressions. The 9-5 is a joke ... it's more like the 8-6. Shift happens and times are a changin.

Risky is the new safe. Getting paid for production is the new show up and punch a time clock. The old we will pay you as little as we can so you don't quit, and you will work just hard enough so you don't get fired is so 2008.

10,000 people a day are turning 65 until 2030. Baby boomers are looking for an encore career. They don't want another job. They certainly don't want to be sending out resumes. Yuck. They'd rather be playing tennis or golf or on a Beach somewhere.

20 somethings coming out of school don't want to be chained to a desk and ... argh no ... pick up a telephone that is actually connected to that desk. They want a life of fun and adventure, they want to tweet and blog and post and get paid for it. They certainly don't want a boss.

We are entering into a production based society. Jobs are being replaced by robots, and foreigners, both immigrants stateside as well as from their homeland, are getting paid pennies for what normally would be high salaried positions. Skilled professionals are getting passed by people half their age, at half their salary.

People are looking for solutions. They want more money yes, but they really want more free time. Your neighbors are stressed out, your colleagues are burnt out, your friends are looking for a better way.

A good job is becoming an oxymoron. I have one friend who went to Yale, highly trained in hospital management and in running medical practices. He has had 2 or 3 jobs since I've know him in only 7 years. It doesn't seem like he ever has enough time in the day ... and certainly doesn't seem so secure in his current gig. My cousin used to own a film and camera shop, the internet put an end to that. He's had 3 or 4 sales jobs since then and hasn't seem to find himself a home. My other friend works for a top finance company and actually makes a lot of money. But after 20 years of commuting 90 minutes one way, he's kinda done with it. Every time I ask him to play golf he's too busy.

So today I sit poolside with a beautiful view and share with you what I've learned. This morning I went for a morning run and did a Facebook live sharing some life lessons I learned on my morning run. The FB live was called (((The Law of Attraction vs The Law of Distraction))) ... it was shot overlooking a beautiful marina. My head was clear after the run and my thoughts were fresh. The ideas were free flowing because I am not an overweight stressed out burnt out dad living for the weekend. From the fb live a lot of my clients, and business partners and friends commented. I got a ton of likes. Now because I'm in flow, I know the likes don't mean anything. Or do they?

Because I added value to the market place, I know have permission to interact with the likes and with the comments. For me to get a like and not respond would be the equivalent of someone going for a high five - when you are in person, and you not responding.

So how do I turn this I to business? Well sometimes I do and sometimes I don't. I'll generally reach out and say something like "thanks for liking my post on the law of attraction, what's new and good with you?"

Now this way I have an opening to engage with folks. Whether they are friends or customers or business prospects I have an easy opening. Then through the art of connection I can continue the dialogue which sometimes leads to business.

Our business is a lifestyle business and we teach people to have a better, well, a better lifestyle. Imagine a triangle. And inside the triangle you have the words "my perfect lifestyle". One leg of the triangle represents better health, one is more income or better wealth and one is more free time - which one (or ones) are you working on?

If you have 2 of the 3, you're almost there - but something is missing. Good health and great income is nice, but without free time it's not all that good. Good health and a ton of free time is kinda cool, but with no money you're missing out. If you have plenty of time and a ton of money but your health is good then clearly you aren't getting the best lifestyle.

Here's the good news. You can have it all. You. Can. Have. It. All.

The laptop lifestyle. More time on the golf course. More time on the beach. More time to travel and pursue your dreams, goals and hobbies. You can even have enough energy to play with you kids.

So. The business choice for millennials. The next chapter for baby boomers. The perfect opportunity for those in between. Let's connect and dig a little deeper. You are ready for more. You want a better life. You are ready to go from good to great. For a one on one, no obligation chat, reach out to me at drewaberman@gmail.com.

For more info check out www.drewberman.com

I look forward to assisting you with your health, wealth and time freedom goals.

CHAPTER 2

BONUS! DOUBLE YOUR INCOME - BUSINESS BUILDER BOOTCAMP - WWW.THELAWOFCOMPENSATION.COM

———

I was going to give this to you as a gift at the end of the book, but most people never even finish the books they buy which is quite sad, but not surprising. Most people don't even read after college. Most people that pick up a guitar don't make it to Madison Square Garden in a Rock Band. Most kids who pick up a baseball bat don't end up playing major league baseball. Most people who start a business don't make millions of dollars. And most people who buy a book don't read it. I know you are going to read it. I'm just talking about other people. So this gift is at the front of the book.

Because I want to show you how to have it all; have more fun, have more impact, and of course make more money.

One of my friends is Maverick Millionaire Paul Finck. He hosts a Double Your Income Bootcamp several times a year around the country. Here you can learn how to network, think bigger, act bigger, be bigger and earn bigger. I have been several times. YOU DESERVE TO GO.

Go to www.thelawofcompensation.com - this will give you elite access to his next upcoming camp. Keep reading for a teaser of what you will find there.

———

DOUBLE YOUR INCOME IN 3 DAYS!

Learn How to Do It Different and Explode Your Income for this year - and Beyond - Over This 3-Day Maverick Event!

Reserve your seats for this upcoming Total Transformation Event at the link below before they are all gone.

Time is Running Out Quickly!!!!

My friend Maverick Millionaire, Paul Finck is ready to show YOU how to Do It Different... and Dare to be a Maverick to create the business and life you have always dreamed about at his upcoming bootcamp.

Normal Price for this event:

$2997.00

Because you are reading this book, we're giving you the VIP treatment.

This is an incredible opportunity for you to spend 3 days on your business and leave with the tools you need to achieve your financial goals this year.

Just go to www.thelawofcompensation.com to reserve your seat today!

The Maverick Way is a different way of thinking and acting in your business. It will separate you from your competition and elevate your results.

The Maverick Way is all about doing it different while having a ton of fun doing it.

You will create tons of energy to feed your vision while leading your team to new heights when you become a Maverick!

Think of some of the great mavericks of our time --->

Sir Richard Branson is an English businessman and investor. He is best known as the founder of Virgin Group, which comprises more than 400 companies. In 1970, he set up a mail-order record business. In 1972, he opened a chain of record stores, Virgin Records, later known as Virgin Megastores. Branson's Virgin brand grew rapidly during the 1980s, as he set up Virgin Atlantic and expanded the Virgin Records music label. In March 2000, Branson was knighted at Buckingham Palace for "services to entrepreneurship". In July 2015, Forbes listed Branson's estimated net worth at US $5 billion.

William "Bill" Gates III is an American business magnate, philanthropist, investor, and computer programmer. In 1975, Gates and Paul Allen co-founded Microsoft, which became the world's largest PC software company. During his career at Microsoft, Gates held the positions of chairman, CEO and chief software architect, and was the largest individual shareholder until May 2014. Gates has authored and co-authored several books. Gates is currently the richest man in the world. Gates is one of the best-known entrepreneurs of the personal computer revolution. Later in his career Gates pursued a number of philanthropic endeavors, donating large amounts of money to various charitable organizations and scientific research programs through the Bill & Melinda Gates Foundation.

Steven "Steve" Jobs was an American technology entrepreneur, visionary and inventor. He was the co-founder, chairman, and chief executive officer (CEO) of Apple Inc.; CEO and largest shareholder of Pixar Animation Studios;a member of The Walt Disney Company's board of directors following its acquisition of Pixar; and founder, chairman, and CEO of NeXT Inc. Jobs is widely recognized as a pioneer of the microcomputer revolution of the 1970s, along with Apple co-founder Steve Wozniak. Shortly after his death, Jobs's official biographer, Walter Isaacson, described him as the "creative entrepreneur whose passion for perfection and ferocious drive revolutionized six industries: personal computers, animated movies, music, phones, tablet computing, and digital publishing."

Jeffrey "Jeff" Bezos is an American entrepreneur and investor. He is a technology entrepreneur who has played a role in the growth of e-commerce as the founder and CEO of Amazon.com, an online merchant of books and later of a wide variety of products. Amazon.com became the largest retailer on the World Wide Web and a model for Internet sales. In 2013, Bezos purchased The Washington Post newspaper.

Andrew Carnegie was a Scottish-American industrialist who led the enormous expansion of the American steel industry in the late 19th century. He built a leadership role as a philanthropist for the United States and the British Empire. During the last 18 years of his life, he gave away to charities, foundations, and universities about $350 million (in 2015, $13.7 billion) – almost 90 percent of his fortune. His 1889 article proclaiming "The Gospel of Wealth" called on the rich to use their wealth to improve society, and it stimulated a wave of philanthropy.

Mark Zuckerberg is an American computer programmer, Internet entrepreneur, and philanthropist. He is the chairman, chief executive, and co-founder of the social networking website Facebook. His personal wealth, as of December 2015, is estimated to be $46 billion. In the spirit of The Giving Pledge, Zuckerberg and his wife Priscilla Chan announced they would give the majority of their wealth over the course of their lives to "advancing human potential and promoting equality". In 2007, at the age of 23, Zuckerberg became a billionaire as a result of Facebook's success. The number of Facebook users worldwide reached a total of one billion in 2012.

What makes them all Mavericks?

They had a vision of a better way to do something

They believed in their idea without fail

They took a chance to make their ideas a reality

They did what others said was impossible

They created worldwide change

Are you ready to become a Maverick just like the ones above?

This is the event to get you started on joining an elite group... the Mavericks in the business world.

Are you looking to:

...attract more clients?

...convert more sales?

...create more profit?

...and double your income?

Learn the unconventional solutions to your SALES challenges at this one of a kind 3-day event where you can Dare to be a Maverick!

Here's some of what you will learn at the 3-day Maverick Selling Business Builder Bootcamp

Top 10 Counter Intuitive Maverick Selling Strategies to double your conversions while creating a higher percentage of prospects to raving fans.

How to tap into the hidden power of your mind to propel you to new levels of greatness in all areas of your life.

The simple process to hypnotize yourself and others quickly to create massive shifts in your life!

Why the wealthiest and most successful people in the world are all

Mavericks... and how you can become one almost immediately.

The easy, fast-analysis, Maverick process to connecting with anyone in minutes to make them feel like you are totally in sync with them. This is VITAL for anyone who deals with prospects, clients, buyers, sellers, contractors - a must for any business owner.

The secrets to choosing the correct team members for every position the way a Maverick does it... and where to find them to fill your team's positions. Mavericks lead the company; their team does the work.

How to grow your business from where it is now to where you want it in the shortest amount of time, the Maverick Way... whether this is just starting out or stepping up to the next level.

The 4 steps Mavericks use to achieve ANY goal in the shortest time possible.

How to take control of any conversation with total confidence and less effort in a matter of seconds. This doesn't mean you talk the whole time. It does mean you control the focus, length and result of your conversations.

The step-by-step process to create yourself as the expert in your field like every Maverick does. You are the go-to person when you master this.

Create real world marketing funnels to produce results... NOW! Mavericks use the latest and best methods to attract new customers... and adopt them quickly to maximize their effectiveness!

Proven Maverick negotiation techniques that will instantly position you better starting TODAY! These are different ways of accomplishing your intended results you have never seen or used this way.

The Maverick Millionaire pulls back the curtain on his own businesses showing you all his Maverick secrets to create the same success he has in his life today.

How to live like a Maverick and "create" your dream world. Mavericks take decisive action to create what they want in their lives instead of accepting what shows up. Are you ready to Maverick up?

And So Much More…

And just in case you wanted even more of a reason to attend this 3-day Maverick Selling Business Builder Bootcamp, here are the Bonuses for you when you attend this special training

BONUS #1: VIP Networking Party -- This is our networking cocktail party with all the VIP attendees at the event. These attendees are the people you want to add to your contact list! Take the time in a relaxed atmosphere to get to know your fellow attendees to see how you are able to help each other out.

BONUS #2: Negotiate Your Life E-book and Audio -- These are some of the great strategies for negotiation provided to you in both audio and written format. These can and should be used regularly to build a great foundation for your persuasion and influence in your everyday life.

BONUS #3: E-Entrepreneur Mindset E-Book - Do you want to have an internet-based business? In today's age, each one of us better be utilizing the internet for our business. This book shows you what it will take to be successful in your E-business.

BONUS #4: Assertiveness E-Book - Are you confident and self-assured in all you do? Am I assertive? Am I too assertive? Am I assertive to the point of being aggressive? This book shows you how to balance your amount of assertiveness to suit the situation you find yourself involved in each moment.

Reserve your spot at the upcoming event.

Just go to www.thelawofcompensation.com reserve your seat today!

Now I know you might be wondering if this event is right for you. This event is for you only when you:

want to double your income this year with a faster & more effective way

enjoy doing it different than all those around you

are ready and willing to make changes in your business now

want more time in your life

are highly motivated and highly interested in changing your life today

readily receive open, honest, constructive feedback about your business

are willing to do Whatever It Takes to create your vision

want a better process or method to take you to your next level

Did you make the cut after those qualifications? I'm guessing yes since you are still reading.

Here's a few more to ensure you are right for the Maverick Selling Business Builder Bootcamp/Total Transformation Event.

This event is NOT for you if you:

are happy where you are right now in your business

get offended easily when you are being coached or mentored

like to do it by the book and follow all the rules

don't want to put the work in necessary to make the changes to get the results you want

only want to grow your business marginally - 10 to 20% - this year like busting your butt all the time leaving you no time to enjoy your life

Still with me?

You are obviously looking for something different in your life.

Other events talk about being different... yet end up covering the same types of information.

The Maverick Selling Business Builder Bootcamp is THE event totally focused on being different - Maverick in every way!!

Nothing happens in any business until someone sells something.

Are you ready to dare to be different... dare to be great?

When you are ready to double your sales, double your free time and double your income, make sure to grab your seat now while they are still available.

Just click on the link below to reserve your seat today!

Reserve Your Seat NOW at www.thelawofcompnesation.com!

If you are still hesitating, read what these people are saying about working with the Maverick Millionaire, Paul Finck:

PAUL B., SOUTHHAVEN, MS

I would absolutely crawl over broken glass to train with Paul Finck. Every time I go spend a week or weekend learning from Paul, I add at least $1,000/month in passive income to my real estate business....and that's been 7 times in the past year and a half. These increases in residual income routinely occur within 1 to 4 weeks of being with him. In fact, the first and also the most recent time I engaged in one of Paul's events, the performance of my real estate investments increased by $2,500/month within weeks of returning with the game plan Paul consistently arms me with. In one year, he helped me move my annual passive real estate income from $30,000 to $175,000.

Paul is authentic, driven, clear, super-helpful, loving, and an absolute results-maker. A master negotiator himself, he has taught me how to discover what others need, communicate effectively, and thereby craft winning deals for both sides of the table. He always equips me with specific, tactical plans to improve my business, as well as general mindset help. More profoundly, he has taught me how to surround myself with people, circumstances, information, and an environment where I'm able to reach many of these successful conclusions myself. Yes, far beyond just giving me a fish, Paul has taught me how to fish so that I may prosper for a lifetime. I recommend anyone willing to do what it takes to succeed to invest whatever time and money is necessary to train with Paul.

KEN T., LOCUST GROVE, VA

"I would recommend this program to the someone looking to graduate from the 95%er to the 5%er of the world. When I put what I learned at this event into action, I will enjoy an increase in income of $2,000,000 this year."

UPDATE: Ken just purchased his second self storage facility.

DREW B., CT

"The most important thing I learned was the 7 Steps to Making Anything Happen. When I put what I learned at this event into practice I will increase my income by $300,000 this year. I would recommend this to anyone who wants to get more out of life, make more money, someone who is in Network Marketing."

PAT M., ORLANDO, FL

"When I put what I learned here into practice, I will enjoy an income of $500,000. I recommend this event to someone who is desiring direction and instruction to transform their life."

LANCE M., ORLANDO, FL

"Because of the weekend I spent and the people I met there I made an extra $2000 the following week! THANKS PAUL"

HEATHER D., FREDERICKSBURG, VA

"Since I started working with you, my entire perception on how to make money has changed. You have expanded my thought processes to the point that I see money and opportunity everywhere! I have created 7 new income streams since we began our journey together and am looking at several more even as I write this. One of the most amazing pieces for me is that many of those opportunities were available to me all along and I simply couldn't recognize the potential to capitalize on them. Thank you so much for your time and dedication to my success!"

B. TOMAYKO, VA

Paul, I would recommend this program to someone who is looking to step up their game. Anyone who has a business, wants to start one or make a change in their life and needs guidance. You and your team helped us not to settle for just comfortable. They showed us how to move out of our comfort zone and how to achieve so much more. What he shows is going to help our business increase by $1.5 million this coming year!"

OWEN W., PUYALLUP, WA

"I would recommend this to someone who is tired of churning from program to program and can't find the secret sauce to make things click."

JENNIFER A., LONG BEACH, CA

"I would recommend this program to someone who is stuck in a mindset that is preventing them from achieving their God-given talent which is holding them back in their life from succeeding.

DAN R., SANTA BARBARA, CA - OWNER, SANTA BARBARA REIA

"I really enjoyed the weekend. It really gave me a clear picture of what I need to do, delegate, delegate, delegate, and place the right people, per your Sunday training, in the right places, on my teams. Thank you Paul. Best training ever!!!"

DAVID S., CHICAGO, IL

"I would recommend this program to someone who wants to get out of their way to create better lives for themself."

S. GLEASON, JOLIET, IL

"The most important thing I learned at this event was understanding myself and how I'm getting in the way to my success. I would recommend it to someone who is stuck in their life."

TAMY, FL

Hi Paul! Thank you so much for your awesome coaching. Your support and encouragement have boosted my self-confidence 100%. Sometimes I feel confused about my direction and you give me the perfect guidance to get back on track and focus. My business is growing and my skills are being fine tuned with your help. I couldn't have done it without you. You are worth every penny!"

JOHN K., ANN ARBOR, MI

"I would recommend this program to someone who wants to achieve more in their life, not only financially, but in all aspects of their life."

SUSAN H., NC

"Paul is the catalyst for my expansion from being an 'inside the box' thinking attorney to my entry into the exciting and creative arena of divorce coaching and public speaking. Without Paul's guidance, I would not have made the leap. His direct and positive approach is exactly what I needed to jump start my career. Paul is an excellent coach and mentor and I highly recommend him."

Teresa V., PA

Thanks to you and your program, my life will never be the same!! I'm definitely not the same person that I was when I met you. When I heard you introduce your program at an event I was attending, I knew I wanted to work with you. However I had a challenge to overcome….I had been burned badly when I bought another program and the person did not follow through. They basically took my money and ran. …I trusted you then with my money, and now I trust you with my life!!!

I never imagined that I would have accomplished the things that I have in what is a relatively short time. Your methods are presented very clearly, and are simple enough for ANYONE who is willing to take direction and ACTION to have major change take place in there life. And, learning from someone who has traveled the road before me in multiple businesses gave me even more confidence in your abilities as a coach.

Our one on one conversations covered so much ground.. I can't even begin to thank you for the guidance and direction you have given me in every area of my life.. from real estate investing, multilevel marketing, and loan repair …to help with improving my relationship with my son. And of course, my biggest challenge….the struggle I have had with losing weight.

I'm extremely happy to say that all areas of my life are greatly improved because of your sincere interest in helping me design my life on purpose!! Because of our work together, my life is more organized, I am more focused, I'm getting lighter, and the future is more clear!! I am living life INTENTIONALLY, and have embarked on a wonderful journey that I may never have taken without your help!!

I thank you from the bottom of my heart !!!!

And if those comments weren't enough,

The Maverick Selling Business Builder Bootcamp/Total Transformation will propel you forward to your next level!

For things to change, you must change.

So ask yourself this key question:

What am I now going to do different to propel myself toward the business success I know I was meant to create?

The Maverick Selling Business Builder Bootcamp/Total Transformation Event

is the starting point to learn how to

Do It Different!

What Are You Waiting For?

Dare to be Maverick!

Reserve your seat at www.thelawofcompensation.com now before they are gone!!

This is an incredible opportunity for you to spend 3 days on your business and leave with the tools you need to achieve your financial goals in this year!

Just go to www.thelawofcompensation.com and reserve your seat today!

CHAPTER 3

BELIEF

The basis of all success begins with belief. You can't begin a new venture into the unknown without certain basic beliefs. In the Network Marketing profession these beliefs are in the Company, the Product, the Compensation Plan, your Support Team, and in yourself.

YOURSELF

The very first thing that you need to believe in is *yourself.* Everyone is capable of success in anything that they dream of doing, given the basic skill set that the dream requires. Not all of us can be a football quarterback, or tennis or golf pro. These dreams require the coordination, skill and stamina that come with the game. We know what we may be capable of in these endeavors. But every one of us has the capability of being successful in the Network Marketing profession! The skills for this game are easy to acquire and become a master at.

All too often we run across people who jump into the business of Network Marketing completely unprepared for what they come up against. In fact, we all start out this way, in any new business. A famous quote comes to my mind, "winners never quit, and quitters never win". That could not be any closer to the truth!

Before you enter this business you should already have made a commitment, not for a few months to 'give it a try', but for at least five years.

The bestselling author Malcolm Gladwell wrote in his book "Outliers: The Story of Success" that it takes 10,000 hours to become a master of something. Let's see, 40 hours a week for 50 weeks times 5…5 years. Why not? If you believe in yourself that much it is a short time, because it is your time invested in your future, and the payoff can be astronomical. Just look at the Beatles! 10,000 hours.

Now that you have made a commitment to yourself that you are going to succeed, and that you are going to give yourself the time it takes to succeed, you need to find the right company.

As we get to know each other and work together we will work on belief. We will also focus on the 3 main components of success in Network Marketing - we will work on the skills, habits and mindset to be successful.

THE COMPANY

Perhaps the hardest thing in this profession is finding the right company to invest your time and energy in. You have to do the research. The way that we typically hear about a Network Marketing company is through a friend or acquaintance. More often than not, we are now finding out about home-based business while browsing online, or from those pre- recorded phone calls.

Regardless of how you find out about a company, you have to understand certain things to fully believe in them. First, who told you about it? Do you trust them? It's a good place to start, but far from the place to dive in. You never know how deep that water really is until you do your own research.

Who founded the company? When? What is the mission statement? What is the profession? There are a lot of companies based on health products, cleaning products, supplements, precious metals, financial plans, the juice of a magic berry, and many, many more. Lose weight from drinking coffee. Drink wine tell friends. Take this growth hormone. And lots more.

Really now! What is the mission statement? Who are the people behind it?

I can't tell you how often I have heard "well the company didn't last" or "my entire downline left in one day". Yes, there are thousands of MLM companies. Do your homework before investing your time and money.

THE PRODUCT

Ah yes. The product. Will drinking a couple of cups of coffee a day that have an extra high level of caffeine and a special 'appetite suppressing' Chinese herb really be the future of the profession? It's doubtful. There are many, many companies that fall into the 'fad' category. There are better choices.

The first question to ask yourself is "would I use this, or consume this, or collect this" product myself, for years to come? The key here is 'for years'. Remember, five years to start. The product line has got to match your lifestyle and belief system. It has to match your potential customers, the people who you will be attracting to you and your offering.

A good way to start is to make a list of all of the things that you get really passionate about. Do you love a clean house? Do you love the process of cleaning?

Do you love to eat right and be as healthy as you can be? Do you want to help others get there? Do you have a great mind for numbers and understand the whims of the financial world? Do you want to help others protect their wealth? Make a list of what is important to you and then look for a company that aligns itself with your beliefs by offering products that you gladly would use and share with others. However. a lot of us were not looking for a company or a business. I was. I was sick of tired of being sick and tired. I knew there had to be a better way. Some, actually most, of your prospects won't necessarily be in the market for a new business or opportunity. Most are exposed to your company via a product introduction.

As we start to work together you will learn the language of this business. You may fall in love with your company and product - and wonder why no one is buying. No worries. We will help you with that.

Often times people feel like the woman in the blue dress. You start your product, you have great results, and people seem to be running away from you or running towards you. Here's a good rule

» something you are doing, or not doing

» is attracting, or repelling people

Too many people get involved, they make their list, they reach out to friends they haven't seen in 20 years, they see their neighbors running away from them, and they don't know why. They are the woman in the blue dress. You see, at the beginning, you have to make up in numbers what you lack in skill. Not that you don't have skill, but it's the skill of this business that takes a minute to learn and a lifetime to master. Blue dress.

For one of the opening seasons for Oprah, she had on the Black Eyed Peas. It was filmed in Chicago, and there was a huge, huge crowd. She came out on stage with BEP and she was so excited. They started to perform and she was so giddy. But as she looked out to the crowd, tens of thousands of people, she only saw one woman dancing, a woman in the blue dress.

This happens in the profession of Network Marketing to often. You sign up and no one signs up with you. You come back from convention and no one returns your phone calls. You are a customer for 7 years, telling everyone you are in business but no one is buying. You are the woman in the blue dress. But as you watch the performance, other people start to join her. Then a few more. Then a few more. Then dozens. Then hundreds. Then thousands. Then the whole place is going wild. It was a surprise for Oprah as they planned a flash mob for her. It's way cool.

Watch the video here - https://bit.ly/2wTEJ2e

This is a great analogy for Network Marketing. It takes a minute to learn and a lifetime to master. You might be the only one dancing at the beginning, but after a while, people will join you, IF, you follow our training - they will join you faster. At the beginning you may not have enough belief, you may have to borrow some from your upline sponsor (or from me your coach). First we will get you dancing, then we will get others to dance with you.

THE COMPENSATION PLAN

This is perhaps the most difficult area for any of us to understand, even after joining a company and starting to live the plan. There are so many creative comp plans. However, creative generally means complex and limited. Gold Stars, Diamond Levels and Platinum Legs; it can all be very confusing.

The way to properly investigate the compensation plan of a company is to get on the phone with someone who really understands it, someone who has been living with it for years and can tell you honestly what to expect. However, this is the exact person who will be attempting to recruit you into the company, so the honesty portion of that concept is dubious at best.

The best advice here is to find a comp plan that is simple, easy to understand, and one that does not limit your possibilities by capping out when you are getting most successful. Many people jump companies after they have met with great success because their comp plan has maxed out. What is the sense of staying around at that point? It can be a difficult decision when the product line fits. Don't get lured in with the belief that you can *start* with this plan, because it will be a long time before I will max out.

That is not believing in yourself. Don't just dabble. 10,000 hours of dabbling is a lot more than five years.

Your company comp plan should be simple to understand, attainable, and rewarding. The average person should be able to get their products paid for in a short time and make a couple hundred a month. Someone who puts in some time and effort should be able to make a car payment or a house payment. A person willing to work on their skills, mindset, beliefs and habits should be able to make a full time income. And some can make millions. If you want to go deeper on this topic reach out to me at www.drewberman.com . I'll help you navigate through these murky waters. We can talk about your current comp plan and how you can do better and achieve more. We can discuss the comp plans of the companies you are researching or I can show you mine. The important thing is we will show you how to win and win big. Not every company has the best product, the best timing, the best executive board and the best comp plan even though a lot claim to. Reach out to me and I will help you.

YOUR SUPPORT TEAM

One of the things that we hear the most from people who have given the business a try, but have not been successful, is that they didn't get true support from their upline team. This probably means that they were unable to give any real support to their downline team, because we all follow the example of those who are doing better at this than we are.

Talk to your potential team. What kind of training do they plan to give to you? Is their system duplicable? What does this really mean? In this book we will talk about the methods that we have spent years developing, weeding out the unsuccessful approaches that we were taught, but spelling out the true systems that have worked over and over again. We are your team.

Nevertheless, your upline is your resource and, hopefully, your guide to success in your company. Your downline is your personal family as such. The bigger the team, the more help comes your way. Use all of the help that you can get. It will cut your learning curve down dramatically. In our group we don't tend to talk upline and downline. We refer to them as support team and success team. We don't just build a business, we build a community. We don't just build a downline, we build a family.

So we are going to work on belief. There is an expression you've heard before - fake it til you make it. I think that is somewhat inauthentic. Let's be of integrity. How about Faith It Til You Make It. Have Faith. Know it will all work out. It may not be easy. No one ever said it would. You gotta believe.

Answer honestly. On a scale of 1-10, rate yourself in belief in the following areas.

1 The Company

2 Network Marketing

3 Your Products

4 Your Support Team

5 Yourself

6 Yourself in Network Marketing

Reach out to me and let me know where your belief level is. I will help you move the needle. Whether you are just getting started, your still looking for a company, or you have been around for awhile - email me at <u>drewaberman@gmail.com</u> and I will help you with belief.

CHAPTER 4

CHOOSING AND GROWING THE TEAM - THE MAGIC IS IN THE 4TH QUESTION

In the field of professional sports, there is not a more stressful position in an organization than the team's general manager. On most teams, the general manager is responsible for assembling the best team possible with the resources provided by ownership.

When the team performs badly, the general manager is criticized by the fans and by his bosses. One poor decision can cost him his job. Therefore, he will carefully weigh every personnel decision to ensure success.

In many traditional business opportunities, success is largely based on how hard you are willing to work, at least in the initial stages. In Network Marketing, the key to success is in building a team of people with similar goals and passion and getting them excited not only about the product, but also about their dreams and goals.

In Network Marketing - you have to wear 3 hats at the same time. First is the General Manager Hat, then the Manager Hat, then the Coaching Hat. General Manager comes first. Your goal is to go out there and find the best team possible. You will learn how to do that with the 4 questions outlined in this chapter. Then once you have a team, you learn to manage them properly. And as you start to grow, you will find 1-5 people to really run with, and to coach them to have the best results possible. I will teach you how to maximize each of these positions.

American industrialist J. Paul Getty once remarked that he would rather have 1% of the effort of 100 people than 100% of the effort of one person. To paraphrase a Verizon Wireless commercial, "It's the network."

In fact, let's get clear with some definitions:

Network (noun): an association of individuals having a common interest, formed to provide mutual assistance, helpful information, or the like, e.g., a network of recent college graduates.

Network (verb): to cultivate people who can be helpful to one professionally, esp. in finding employment or moving to a higher position, e.g., his business lunches were taken up with networking.

Marketing (noun): the total of activities involved in the transfer of goods from the producer or seller to the consumer or buyer, including advertising, shipping, storing, and selling.

Because I am a student of the Law of Attraction, I believe we attract who we are, not necessarily who we want to be. Mahatma Gandhi once said, "Be the change you want to see in the world." I say lets be the change you want to see in the Network Marketing Profession. Be the leader, be the trainer, be the executive, whom others would want to be, and also whom others would want to follow.

One of my friends and mentors, Lenny Evans, says this: "Be the leader that leaders are looking for." In my Network Marketing company, one of our goals is to become an Executive. I teach my teams, "Before you can become an Executive – you have to *BE* an executive."

One of the formulas I study is "be, do, have." I think some people focus on either having things or the lack of having things. They focus on what they want and what they do not have. Some people focus on the doing of things, and they do, do, do – they are in constant action. Perhaps you can picture the businessman in a suit running full speed on a treadmill.

My question is, who are you being so that what you are doing becomes effortless and what you are having becomes inevitable. In other words, are what you say, what you do and what you want all in alignment?

As I see it, there are four essential questions that you must ask when you are in the process of looking for associates (I have also included my answers. I recommend you answer them for yourself to assist you on your journey).

The best way to get the most out of this is to write this out somewhere important. Perhaps in your success journal, on a piece of paper you hang on your wall or by you bed. Keep it somewhere you can reference it often, I recommend at least 2 times a day. Write the 4 questions out, and leave some space between them. Read the questions a few times so they really sink in. Answer the questions in a different color so they stand out. The magic is in the 4th question. If you answer this truthfully, it will unlock the Law of Attraction in your favor. You will become the person you are looking for. You will then attract the person you are looking for, and the person you are looking for, is looking for you. First we are going to find people in your warm market, then we are going to find people in your cold market, and then we are going to attract people to you. This takes a minute to learn and a lifetime to master. Answering these 4 questions honestly will short cut your success. Treat this activity seriously and magic will happen in your life and business.

WHO ARE MY IDEAL ASSOCIATES?

You must visualize them in your mind and know what to look for before you start looking. When you go to a restaurant, the waitress will hand you a menu and then you will order what you want. Take the opportunity before you start prospecting to ask yourself what you want in an associate. Who are you looking for? How do you identify them when you cross paths with them?

My ideal associates and clients are healthy (or they want to get healthy) and they are professional. They are interested in good, vibrant health and live the image (or want to life the image) of good health. They are working professionals, interested in wealth and abundance. They are open-minded, like to read, are interested in networking, and enjoy helping people. They are parents, teachers, mentors, entrepreneurs, athletes, chiropractors, networkers and network marketers. They are active military or veterans. My ideal associates want more out of life. They are A+ players stuck in a B game. They are winners, movers and shakers, and they want to win and win big. They are sick and tired of being sick and tired or they are already super successful and the want more. They are Mom or DadPreneurs. They know they have game they just need the right guidance or the right vehicle. They have had some success in their life and they want to duplicate it. If this is you or someone you know - send me an email at drewaberman@gmail.com.

WHERE ARE MY IDEAL ASSOCIATES?

Your ideal associates are anywhere and everywhere. Now that you have identified your ideal prospects – where do you find them? They may very well be the waiter or waitress that takes your order and goes the extra mile to make your meal more enjoyable. The key is looking at people through the lens of your opportunity and seeing who is in focus. Do not confuse that with constantly "prospecting" everybody – just keep your eyes open.

I find new associates at financial seminars, BNI meetings, Chamber of Commerce meetings, my house of worship, the bank, post office, and the YMCA. They may currently be in my Rolodex. Maybe I went to high school with them. I went to college with them. They were in my fraternity. They are in my business community. They are at the supermarket and in my path when I am out and about. They are the business owners in my neighborhood and the parents at my children's school. They are on Facebook and LinkedIn. They attend wealth retreats and networking events. I might find some at the next Tony Robbins Event.

WHAT MAKES THEM TICK?

This is a very important question. If you do not know what they are all about, what they think about and what they want, how could you possibly help them?

This business has nothing to do with you, your compensation plan, your product or how great your executive board is. They care about WIIFM – what's in it for me? Who are you? What can you do for me? Can you solve my problems? In order to answer these questions, you must ask them, and then be open to receive the answers.

What do your prospects (let's call them new friends or potentially new associates) think about? What do they read? Where do they spend their days off? With whom do they associate? Do they want to retire their spouse? Where do they like to vacation? Are they looking for a new car? Ah yes, what makes them tick? If you do not know what makes them tick, you are nothing but a salesman.

Here is my answer for that question:

They are well read, well spoken, and professional. They like to ski in exotic places, play golf, and read books by Robert Kiyosaki, Jeffrey Combs, T. Harv Eker, and Jack Canfield, Ray Higdon and Eric Worre.

They have goals in life. They want to let their spouse stay at home with the kids and send those kids to the best private schools and colleges. They want to pay down debts, pay off the mortgage a little faster, take that nice vacation they've been promising themselves, or make that major purchase they've been eyeing for years.

They may not know what they need to do, but they intuitively understand that what they are currently doing isn't cutting it. Or, they are already successful and want to go to the next level. Therefore, they are actively seeking an opportunity to gain financial freedom without mortgaging time with their families.

In short, they are motivated, goal-oriented people who believe strongly in self-improvement. Give them the right product and outstanding support and they will take themselves (and you) to new heights in the business.

The people I look for have 6 key skills – the ability to: recruit, enroll, train, motivate, manage and present.

WHAT DO I NEED TO DO, CHANGE OR IMPROVE TO ATTRACT MORE OF THEM?

These four questions can help you find your mate, your job, your business opportunity, your employees, or your new business associates, but this question is vital! This is perhaps the most difficult question to answer, because it requires us to admit that we aren't perfect the way that we are.

Let's assume your comp plan works, your product is amazing, and you love your company – the only missing ingredient, my friend, is you. As you change, you grow. As you grow, you start attracting new and different people into your life.

Most people tend to talk to their immediate demographic when they start. I recommend you seek out the most successful people you know;

the ones that are already successful will be successful in this endeavor. The ones that are not yet successful will have to learn the skill sets of a successful person.

Wouldn't you agree?

You need to be what you want your associates to be.

For myself, I have to be goal-oriented and driven to success. I want to win my company's recruiting contests. I need to successfully mentor my downline and share what I have learned about this business. My commitment to my team and myself requires that I continue to learn and to study. I need to be well dressed, neatly shaven, and a leader in my community. I need to do community service, help at my sons' school, and donate my time and money. I have to study from the millionaires in my profession. I have to be well read and attend leadership seminars.

Because my product line is health and wellness related, I need to be in great shape. I also need to be a great husband and father so that my personal life is gratifying and I achieve balance.

Attracting the right associates requires the commitment to be the right associate. We attract who we are.

I recommend that you stop reading right now, write down these 4 questions on piece of paper (one that you will not lose – either put it in your day planner or your ongoing success journal), and then answer them in a different color. Make sure you have all the answers on one piece of paper. Read it often – at least once in the morning and once at night. If you do this, magic will happen!

Before you continue, take an opportunity to review. What did you get out of this chapter? Do not let the simplicity of these principles fool you. I bet if you take them seriously and track your success for 90 days, you will see a dramatic improvement.

CHAPTER 5

8 STEPS TO SUCCESS

―――――

Network Marketing is a business. It is also a game. It can be fun. It can be very lucrative. Success takes certain characteristics, no matter what profession you are in. What does it take to succeed in Network Marketing? It takes dedication, commitment, focus, energy, leadership-ability, coach- ability, time management, patience, and more. We can guide you to resources to improve in all of these areas, but you have to self-assess where you are strong and where you are weak. You will also have to do this for the teams that you develop. Once you have the desire and you are ready to take massive action, then we can guide you to success.

Success is a process. Network Marketing is a process. This eight step process can help you to get the results that you wish to achieve. Each step can take seconds to learn, years to practice, and a lifetime to master. Any skill can be learned. Any learned skill can be mastered. Every master was once a disaster, my mentor David Wood says often.

Have you have heard the expression "sponsor up"? What does that mean? Well, you want to get good at identifying smart people who already have had some success. Chances are that they will bring their talents with them when they join your team. Can people who are not successful, who do not manage their time well, who do not have leadership skills, be successful in your business? Yes, of course, but let us ask it this way. Do you want people who are not successful, who do not manage their time well, who do not have leadership skills in your business?

Most people tend to sponsor people in their own demographic. This is very limiting. Sponsor up! Sponsor Up! SPONSOR UP! If you drag broke and tired people, who are sick and complaining, into your business, because they need your product, and they need your comp plan, then you will have a team of broke, tired and sick people.

That being said, you still want to see the best in people. I have a plaque on my desk that reads, "when I let go of what I am, I become what I might be", a saying by Lao Tzu. It's the same thing with your team and future teammates. Believe in who they can be, don't limit them by who they are. Speak greatness into people and you will have raving fans.

Show people a glimpse of the future, give people a sneak peak into their potential and watch as miracles happen. This is an art; look at the gradient (later chapter). Don't promise people riches and fame and time freedom if they have not yet developed the skill sets needed.

When we are in alignment with what we do, what we want and what we say, magic will happen. When one is committed, providence happens.

This may take weeks or months, or years, or decades - but it is worth it. Network Marketing deserves your attention. Even if you just want to make an extra $1,000 a month. However, if you want to make big money, let's call it six figures, there is a process that we recommend. Let's just pause for a second for a mental check in. Did you read that last sentence and think six figures a year, or did you read that last sentence thinking six figures a month? Hmm, just something to think about. What kind of story are you writing for yourself? Either way, both numbers are attainable.

This business ultimately has a lot less to do with your product and your comp plan then you think. It has to do with moving people into action. I learned 20 years ago, when I was Social Chairman of my fraternity (Pi

Kappa Alpha) at George Washington University, how difficult it is to get people into motion. You would think that the main reason people join a fraternity is for the social aspect, and yet it was still challenging to get people moving. The same thing goes for Network Marketing. At first you are faced with motivating just one person to take action and make a decision. Then you get to do that over and over. So if you spend some time and focus on the process, you can have great results in Network Marketing. This process has made me a lot of money and can make you a lot of money as well.

THE EIGHT STEPS REVEALED

These eight steps, when learned and then, eventually, mastered, can make or break your experience in Network Marketing. Each step is a process in itself and deserves your attention. First we will list the steps, then we will go a bit deeper.

The 8 step process to 6 figures in Network Marketing:

1. Stranger to Hello

2. Hello to Are You Open

3. Are You Open to an Appointment

4. Appointment to Presentation

5. Presentation to Objections

6. Objections to Follow Up

7. Follow Up to Enrollment

8. Enrollment to Advancement

STRANGER TO HELLO

Without this step we can't even begin. Ironically, it's this step that stops most people. Most people in Network Marketing don't ever sponsor even one person. That's right. They have raised their hand, they have said that they want to make money, and they can't even get out of the gate. We can do a whole weekend course on how to approach people. Whether you are making contacts offline or online, we are in a people business, and no people - no business! Step one is affectionately called prospecting. No prospecting - no business. *Know* prospecting - *know* business.

Pick a business: carpenter, doctor, lawyer, dentist, florist, car dealer; you need people. People to buy your product or service and, more importantly, people for you to serve. You are in business now. You need to find customers and you need to find business partners. Some of the people you present to will be people you already know and others will be people that you don't know. Yet, which group has more people, those that you know or those you don't know?

So your first skill it to learn how to approach people you already know, your warm market. Then you have to learn how to meet people when you are out and about. This is prospecting. Remember, and this is very important, you don't go out to prospect, you prospect while you are out. Then you learn how to market, online and offline, so that people come to you. When you have more leads then time, you are in a good position. So as part of step 1 you have to develop your list.

Your List

Old school networkers will tell you to make a list of 100 people. We say to make a list of 10. Also, don't tell your new people to go out and make a list, they don't know how and then you may never see them again.

Book appointments with your new teammates, or the new members of your community, and help them to make a list.

When I refer to the word stranger, I am referring to people who are a stranger to your business, who could be people you have never met before, your cold list, or people you may already be in contact with in some way, your warm list. Your warm list may or may not be the best set of people to approach at first.

There are a lot of factors to be considered. How confident are you? Did you have good product results? Do you have a large sphere of influence? Are you somewhat introverted? Are you new to Network Marketing? Are you a seasoned veteran in a business? Do you have influence in your community? Do you have a history of being successful?

For me, I could not get anywhere with my first company, Amway, even after five years. I couldn't get results from my warm market or my cold market. In my current company, I couldn't go near my warm market, because they were judging me from their prior experience of my approaching them, but when I started having success with people I did not know, some, and only some, of my warm market started coming around.

Stranger to Hello. This is so important. Sometimes you have to start with hello, literally. Hi. Nice day.

How are things? What's new and exciting? You might be laughing at how basic this is or you might be getting sweaty palms at the mere thought of this.

Either way, you will have people in your group, on your team, in your community, that don't even know how to talk to people. We can teach you what to say, but it's not the words you say, it's the music you play.

One of my friends and teammates is a musician. He showed me how to hold the guitar and twist my hand and my little pinky so that I can properly reach the strings. Even that part was painful for me. So, to really get into prospecting, list building, connecting with people online and offline, we are going to need to spend some time together. Here are some resources that I recommend.

Your first resource is at www.drewberman.com. Go there daily, if not weekly, a wealth of professional content. Your next resource is my free -trainings on Youtube.com There you will find the most cutting edge training for both online and offline marketing.

I have a lot of friends who are super successful in Network Marketing - over the years I have gotten the opportunity to work with and study with some of the legends of our time. I have been blessed to work with and or train and learn from;

MJ Durkin – known as America's Prospecting Coach and author of "Double Your Contacts". MJ teaches what to say and what not to say.

Mike Dillard - the father of Attraction Marketing and author of "Magnetic Sponsoring".

Don Spini - author of bestselling "60 Seconds to YES". This is phenomenal training.

Eric Worre - author of GoPro

Ray Higdon - Founder of RankMakers.

and many many others. And if you have not yet registered for the upcoming Double Your Income Bootcamp - I highly recommend you do that now at www.thelawofcompensation.com

And now I give you the best of the best.

So now that you have said hello, you have made small talk, gotten to know each other and caught up on old times. Now you transition to Are you Open?

HELLO TO ARE YOU OPEN

We must find a want, need or desire before moving ahead with people. Most people will just go right into the sales mode here. Big mistake! Our advice? Stop selling! Start connecting. Sell less, connect more.

We have what they want, right? Our products work, our comp plan works. So what is the problem? It is time to find out: what is their pain and what is their pleasure?

What can your product, idea or service do for them, how can it benefit them and how can it help them in their life? If you don't know these answers then you are merely a salesman and may convert 1 in 10, if you *convince* them. This will greatly limit your success. Are they even open to hearing what you have to offer? Open, meaning are they open minded to hearing what you have to offer. Have you created a curiosity? You have to wait until they ask you for information. You can't just launch into your presentation. This is the biggest mistake that people make, and it will blow away your prospect, pretty much all of the time.

Once you are asked for the presentation, are you planning to lead off with your product? Are you going to tell them how great you feel on your product that you are using and about how you are excited for them to try it too? Or are you leading with a business opportunity? I have found that while people might not be interested in the business, they may still be open to the product. It's all in the language. I do not present a business opportunity, per se (what do you think of when you hear someone start in with 'this is a great business opportunity'). Most people will think about how busy they already are, or their existing business requirements. I always present my business as an extra stream of income.

This takes a lot of practice, but when you get good at it, people will come to you having already decided 'yes'. It is time to stop chasing; stop convincing.

Identify a want, need or desire in your prospect. Learn how to find out what people's problems are and how to solve them with your offering, but don't verbally vomit on them. But, we are getting ahead of ourselves.

As a beginner, we tend to mush all of the steps together. We encourage you to be distinct in your communication and to know your intentions and expectations. Keep a chart of these steps and then gently guide people through the process. As a seasoned veteran, we tend to mix the steps up. It's kind of like playing jazz. Once you know the notes, the tune, and the harmony, you can improvise and it will sound unique; it will be your own. People will sign up with you. But if you improvise it too soon, without really knowing the steps, it will sound like noise, not music. People will not sign up with you because they will be confused. Awareness is the first step toward change.

ARE YOU OPEN TO APPOINTMENT

Ah, now this is high-level training. Step 3 can be the difference between a couple of grand a month and a couple of grand a week. We think this is where most people miss the boat; they miss the big picture. If you have gotten steps 1 and 2 down pat, you are well on your way. You are further along than most. You are probably taking this business seriously and you are looking to grow yours. You probably have some success under your belt and you want to have more. Most people go right from step 2 to step 4, and this is a big, a huge, mistake. If this is not done right it will turn off and turn away a lot of people. More people will say No instead of Yes and you won't know why.

Step 3 is critical. You have to make an appointment.

Remember, *you teach people how to treat you.* You do this by how you act and communicate on a regular basis. You teach your spouse how to treat you, your kids how to treat you, and your prospects how to treat you. Let's not call them prospects. Let's call them new business partners, new customers, new team members or, better yet, new members of your community. You are not just building a team; you are building a community. You want to be successful, right? You want others to be successful, right? Then build a community.

To add fuel to your fire after step 2, let's practice making an appointment. Sound simple? Sound basic? Logical? Intimidating? None of the above? All of the above? Remember, you are reading this for *you*, as a student. You are also reading this to become a teacher, mentor and influencer of people. If you are at step 2 with someone and have developed interest or curiosity and you VV them (verbally vomit all of your product info all over them), then you are "that sales person doing another one of those things". You have lost them. You just shoved all your CDs and brochures in their face and then they said they want to think about it. Did you see their attention start to wander? Their eyes start to drift?

Their polite smile? That is because you just figuratively threw up on their shoes. Would you want to do business with someone that threw up on your shoes?

You've probably been to a party, personal or professional, or some kind of networking event, and you were handed a bunch of business cards, or someone just spent 10 minutes telling you what they do. Or perhaps you are on Facebook and you see someone's profile pushing his or her super juice of the month. I know this is not you. You are a professional. You are a professional network marketer. You market a good product and/or service and you are willing to talk about it at the right time and place. Make the appointment.

Here is another scenario. Your prospect said that they would look at your info. They would review your website. You said "GREAT" because you "GOT ONE", like you just went fishing. WOO HOO, you tell your wife, or your husband, or your upline or, even worse, yourself. You think that you have got yourself a prospect – which then turns into a suspect. You tell them you'll call them in a couple of days, and then they join the witness protection program and won't return any of your calls. Then they end up on your never ending, 'shame-on-you', eternal list of people who are in MaybeLand, who suck all of your time and energy, and you can't figure out why they have unfriended you on Facebook – but they were interested, right?

Wrong!

Do you tell your doctor that you will swing by? Does your lawyer say "come to my office in a couple of days and we can follow up"? When do you go to the dentist - sometime soon? You are a professional just like all of them. You are either part-time or full-time, but either way, you are busy. You are a busy executive. They are busy as well. You don't want to get into voicemail Hell, do you? Step 3 is so important. It's so easy, and it's so lucrative. You've got their attention; they have expressed interest or curiosity and asked for more information. At least they are open. Great. Well done. "Now, when can we chat?" This question will make you a lot of money.

We should go a little deeper here. Are you setting an appointment to *sell* them your product or service, or are you meeting with them because you have identified a need, want or desire and you have a potential solution. This approach is what separates amateurs from professionals.

This will help you go from good to great. Applying this philosophy will help you get from where you are to where you want to be.

How do you make appointments? By asking questions like,

»   when is a good time to follow up?

»   when can we spend some time together on the phone where you will not be interrupted?

»   is it better to reach you in the morning or afternoon? What day?

What time?

Or-by telling them when you are available.

»   I can speak to you on Tuesday or Thursday, which is better for you?

I have 1pm or 3pm open.

After you have an appointment, confirm by an email with an action step.

"It was great to chat with you the other day. I look forward to continuing our conversation on Tuesday at 4pm, as we discussed. Can you be in front of a computer when I call? That will make our time together more productive. Also, will you please watch this video about how we have helped others in your situation?

If anything comes up that would require you to reschedule, can you please email me so that I can give the timeslot to someone else and prioritize another time with you in my calendar?"

Step 3 is so important!

APPOINTMENT TO PRESENTATION

Your presentation can be done in a number of ways. The most common ways in Network Marketing are: a video, an audio overview, a 3-way call, a webinar, a teleconference, a one-on-one meeting, a house presentation, a group or hotel presentation. Let's assume that, whether you are new to this game or you are a seasoned pro, you know how to do your company presentation. Yet, it's the language, the posture and the energy that you have in the conversation *before* the presentation, and what you do and say (and what you don't do and say) *after* the presentation, that will make you a fortune in our profession.

The presentation needs to be as short as possible. If you understand your prospective buyer's needs and wants clearly, then you know what you have to say. You should keep your presentation as short and to the point as possible. Have you ever been a witness called to the stand? Do you just ramble on and on spouting unrelated information? Hopefully not! The thing to keep in mind here is that your prospect has already said 'yes' to themselves, which is why they are willing to listen, and want to say 'yes' to you, so the only thing that you can do here is to dampen their enthusiasm with too many words. There is a quote that goes "seek not to know all of the answers, only to understand the questions". How right is that? You have two ears and one mouth, so you should be listening twice as much as you are speaking…or more!

Once you have answered their questions – your presentation – there are two very powerful follow up questions you can ask:

Question #1: After hearing the presentation, what interested you most, a product experience or the income opportunity?

For my business, my exact question is "what interested you more, better health, better wealth, or both?"

Question #2: After reviewing our program, how would you like to see our company (product, service, team) benefit you and help you in your life?

These two questions, when asked properly, can be game changers.

PRESENTATION TO OBJECTIONS

Very rarely do people really say 'No'. They are ready to say 'Yes' when you began. They often say no because they don't *know*, which can lead to objections. Let's call them questions. Questions are easier to handle then objections.

If people say no, no thanks, not interested, or any other variation, this is a good thing. On the list, off the list – no pressure. Yes or no, I've got to go, this a- train is a-movin'! Small list, big objections, big problems, big pressure – small business. Large list, fewer objections – big business. If you have a list of three people and someone has a lot of questions, you are going to spend a lot of time with this person. If you have a list of 300, you will learn how to cull out the best. If you have less then 25 people on your list, you don't have an objection problem, you have a lack of people problem. When the late great Jim Rohn was asked where he found his people, he said, "Wherever they are".

Ironically, you will generally attract the questions (objection) that you are having the most trouble with yourself. If you think that it is hard to make money, since you didn't get in at the ground floor of the company, or whatever, that is what you will attract. If you are having trouble with the cost of your product, then people will tell you it is too expensive.

Objections and questions are part of the process. They are not saying 'no', they are saying "I need more information before I can say yes". If they say a true no, bless them and release them. In fact, I encourage people to say no.

Here's a good example. "When we meet for our appointment (taken from the very important often neglected step 3), if I show you a potential solution and it is not a good fit, will you please be honest and tell me 'no' upfront?" (I say this while nodding my head yes...even when I am on the phone) Yes, I will tell you 'no'.

Great! Now if the objections come, you know they want to say 'yes'. Answer their questions. Get them more information. Tell them about your unconditional money back guarantee. Then say, "Have I given you enough information to at least give it a shot"? That is your leading question!

Use the tools. Show them where they can find the answer. I rarely show the comp plan. I guide them to the comp plan video. I rarely get into ingredients. I send them to the Doctor video or the website.

OBJECTIONS TO FOLLOW UP

Here is the whole section on follow up. It's simple. It's important. It's necessary. It's part of our game.

You must follow up! So, here is the wisdom and the depth; the entire section. Ready? It's deep. Profound actually. Got a pen? Follow Up!! Make the calls!

Call them until you have a definite Yes or No! Get them off of your list. Most people stop after one or two follow up calls. Most prospects don't enroll until the fourth or fifth follow up call. Truth!

FOLLOW UP TO ENROLLMENT

They have said 'yes'. They want to join. They are excited, eager and willing. Their credit card is actually out of the wallet. Do you know how many people actually blow it right here? Yup... they can't sell themselves out of a paper bag and they actually convince people to *not* join their company, their team, their shriveling little empire —no one wants to join.

Why? Some people fear success and some fear failure. They have one extended hand, palm facing up, asking the world for all of it's blessings, but their attitude, or vibration, or energy, has the other hand as a stop sign, telling the universe 'don't trust me, don't give me money don't join my team'. Remember, most people who say yes to Network Marketing never sponsor their first person. It's all in the posture!

One great method for enrolling a new person who is ready to go is to send them an email with a sheet of a step-by-step process of enrolling, answering all of their questions *before* they get to these decision points during the enrollment, and then point them to the 'Sign Up and Save' button on your website, either in the email or on while you are on the phone with them. Let them do it themselves, but guide them there while you are on the phone with them, take them to the button and have them press it. You can stay on with them, but don't VV all over them now! If you teach them to do the process themselves, that is what they will teach others, without the fear of the unknown. Everyone is unsure when they are signing up, because they don't want any hidden commitments that may be diffculti to break. Reassure them and let them do their own thing.

ENROLLMENT TO ADVANCEMENT

So, back to step 8: Enrollment to Advancement. Most people don't understand the sales process. They think the sales process ends when people say yes to your product or opportunity. These are short sighted people, non-visionaries, and they will limit their own growth in Network Marketing.

When someone signs up, enrolls, or joins your growing community - this is when the sales cycle starts. The definition of sponsoring is to take responsibility for your new business partner. Help them, don't enable them. Challenge them, don't alienate them. Encourage them without doing it for them. An old proverb says, "Give a man a fish, feed him for a day. Teach a man to fish, feed him for a lifetime." Get it? We go into a lot more detail on team building and leadership at www.drewberman.com.

AFTERTHOUGHTS

Here is a review of the eight steps;

1) Step 1 - Stranger to Hello – you have got to talk to people. You have to, at least, begin the journey.

2) Step 2 - Hello to Are You Open - you have to create curiosity, develop rapport, and stop selling and convincing; focus on contributing and serving.

3) Step 3 - Are You Open to Appointment - making the appointment is the key to success.

4) Step 4 - Appointment to Presentation - if you can do the other seven then you should be able to do this. If you can't call your upline and if they are of no help, then visit me at www.drewberman.com - everyone needs a coach, and I am available.

5) Step 5 - Presentation to Objections- if you do the other steps properly, you are a student of the game, you have vision, commitment, leadership skills and you are in love with your company and your product, you will have less and less objections as you go down this

journey. At the beginning you have to make up in numbers what you lack in skills. That will change as you and your team (and the community you are building) all grow.

6) Step 6 - Objections to Follow Up - the 6th step is the 6th most important step, hey, what can I say?

7) Step 7 - Follow Up to Enrollment - you have to be professional, you have to expect greatness, you have to help people finish the deal, you must ask for the order. The way you enroll them will be the way they enroll others.

8) Step 8 - Enrollment to Advancement - if you want to make big money, you have to learn how to advance people up the ranks and into higher pay

Here is a self-assessment. On a scale of 1-10, 10 being very strong and 1 being not very strong, where do you rate yourself in each step?

1. Stranger to Hello

2. Hello to Are You Open

3. Are You Open to Appointment

4. Appointment to Presentation

5. Presentation to Objections

6. Objections to Follow Up

7. Follow Up to Enrollment

8. Enrollment to Advancement

Identify your strengths. Use them wisely. Identify your weaknesses and become a student. Learn this process. Master it. Teach it. You will grow bigger, deeper and faster then you have ever imagined. This is the foundation of prospecting and recruiting. Learn, implement and teach these concepts and your business will grow. They seem simple to some, complex to others. Master the basics. Keep it simple. Teach it often. If you want to explore further on this process reach out to me at <u>dbi@drewberman.com.</u>

CHAPTER 6

STOP SELLING - START SERVING

___

No friends. No Business. *Know* friends. *Know* business. That's it. Period. This business is about relationships. How deep can you develop relationships? Friendships and relationships; both action words. They end in ships... ships are meant to be in motion. I'll never forget one of the old Amway tapes. That's right, tapes. I had a collection of tapes before CDs, mp3s and podcasts. I have been educating myself in this profession for nearly 20 years. I recommend that you do the same. In Amway, one of the goals was to "go Platinum". There was a tape I used to listen to called "Friendship before Platinum-ship"...

Build the relationship before you build the business.

Stop selling. This is a big problem in our profession. Yes, you can utilize sales skills. Yes, you can be super successful without ever being exposed to sales, but this is not a business about selling. Most people sell, sell, sell. Even on Facebook. Stop that. You are not your company. You are not your product. You may make some money selling; you might be able to be successful, to a point, by selling your product. You might have a really great product that everyone wants to buy. But it's the relationships that will get you from where you are to where you want to be.

There are 5 ways to keep people loyal, to have them stick around for the long term.

___

1. a good product experience

2. a quick financial gain

3. getting people exposed to a winning team, a fun environment, a community

4. helping people achieve what they want

5. developing a deep friendship

Three, four and five are all about relationships. When you focus on one of the five you might have someone that will stick around. If you help people with more than one there is a good chance they will be on your team for a while. When you focus on all five, you will have fans, raving fans, for a long, long time. You will have a thriving team, a community in which people want to be involved in.

You know that you will have everything in life that you want if you help enough people get what they want.

Focus on people. Focus on helping people. Yes, you can use sales skills to show people that when they use your product or service it will benefit them in some way. This is professional. No problem there.

But if you use sales skills (or sales *techniques* – yuck yuck yuck) then you are being manipulative, which is not cool. It goes back to the gradient. If you promise people huge money and time freedom and you do not take them down the path, guide them down all the challenges and victories, show them by example how and what to do, then you have merely convinced them to join, and they will quit before you can even get them going. A person convinced against their will is of that same conviction still.

Make friends. Enhance people's lives. Surround yourself with people you love, or people you are willing to grow to love. When your best friends are part of your business, and your business is part of your life, then your organization will grow bigger and faster than you could ever imagine. There are some people that you can work with, and there are some people that you have to work through. You might not connect with everyone on your team. Make sure someone does. Introduce people on your team, or people soon to join your team, to other members of your community. It takes a village to raise a child. It takes a community to develop a long lasting thriving business. That is what you want right? Why does it take a community? Because, you can't be best friends with everyone in your organization.

Upline, downline, crossline... stop using this vocabulary. How about support team, success team, partner, friend.

When you say, "meet my upline" they think, "this guy makes money from me". Really? Yes, really. That is what they think. This is a big problem with 3-way calls as well. When done properly, 3-way calls can add value to your community, create a thriving business, and help you make a lot of money. When done improperly, 3-way calls can scare off your new people. The 3-way call is another form of relationship building. When you have a new team member, introduce them to someone on their support team.

Help them become friends. Teach your new people to reach out to people in their "upline" to develop relationships. Its OK if the relationships begin with an umbrella of business. It is OK if they progress, because of business, into friendships. Of course, friendships cannot be forced, but they can be *nurtured*. Nurture your relationships and they will grow deep. Deep relationships will help you grow a deep business.

There are some people in my organization that I will never be friends with. There are some people on my team, folks within my community, who actually do not like me. They don't return my phone calls, they don't come to events, they certainly don't respond to emails. That's OK. I can't be liked by everyone. On the other hand, some of my best friends on the planet are my business partners.

Those relationships run deep. They run deep personally, they run deep professionally, and they run deep in the organization.

When you develop relationships 4 levels deep you are set for a huge business in Network Marketing.

Potentially, you will build a business that will last forever. You sponsor Jon who sponsors Joe who sponsors Susan who sponsors Mary. You plus four levels... Jon - Joe -Susan - Mary. Four levels deep. If you are best friends with these four, you care about their family, you invite them over socially, and you nurture a relationship beyond the fact that you are business partners, then your business is solid. In most companies, regardless of comp plan, people are linked together when they are on the same leg. If you focus on developing relationships, 4 levels deep, in each of your legs, and you teach your teammates, your community members, to do the same, then you will have a strong, balanced, profitable business. You will create a community of like-minded individuals, going strongly after the same goals, dancing to the same beat, and you will be unstoppable.

CHAPTER 7

THE POWER OF YOUR 30-SECOND STORY

───────

You may be asking yourself, "Why should I create a 30-Second story? Why not a one-minute or five- minute presentation complete with a foolproof pitch that will convince everyone who hears it that my product works?"

To answer these questions, we should first break down the three main components of this powerful marketing tool:

It has to be YOURS It has to be SHORT It has to be WELL TOLD

FIRST, IT HAS TO BE YOUR STORY.

On the surface, that seems obvious, but it bears mentioning, because any business you choose to devote your precious time and energy to must have earned your own authentic endorsement in your own words. Otherwise, you will not be believed. When you believe, you become believable. (Unless you are at the very beginning of using a new product or creating a new business, in which case you can borrow the successful story from me or from one of your upline leaders or your other partners in the business.)

The world is full of examples. In a presidential election campaign, the candidate who tells (or appears to tell) his or her story in his or her own words is generally considered to be the most believable. When a person giving remarks is obviously reading them from a page or a teleprompter, it may appear disingenuous.

More than having a product or service to sell, you first have a story to tell. Your very own story, completely unique from anyone else's on the planet. We like to put it this way: "Facts tell, stories sell."

SECOND, IT HAS TO BE SHORT.

As you consider the message behind your story you must bear in mind that people in the 21st century have drastically shortened attention spans. To utilize the political campaign analogy, we are not so much interested in the hour-long speech as we are in the

15-or 30-second sound bite. One of the people I have studied was a Los Angeles morning-drive DJ named Joel Roberts. He is the one that taught me about sound bites. He said if you do not grab your audience in 8-15 seconds, then they are gone!

News outlets, such as CNN, Fox, and MSNBC, cater to this tendency. When the news anchors deliver top stories every hour, at best they will devote no more than five minutes of airtime to any one story.

Therefore, they summarize the most important details, throw in a couple of sound bites from the location where the event has occurred, and move on to the next story.

As a society, we have been programmed to process information this way. Therefore, we should apply this principle to the story we tell about our product.

THIRD, IT MUST BE WELL TOLD.

In order to be told well, your story must be practiced. "Wait!" You may say to yourself, "Shouldn't I just tell my story the way it comes out, in my own words, and let it be "'natural'"?

By all means, be natural and authentic. Speak from the heart. But as time goes on, you will want to practice. In sales they call the 30 -second story your "elevator pitch", because in an elevator you usually have only one chance to get your point across and it usually happens in about 30 seconds. Here's another way to look at it... how about your HOT TUB pitch. Chilling out, at your favorite vacation spot, relaxing, little fruity drink in your hand. When someone comes in and ask what you are up to … you can share your 30 second story.

In the same way, you will often have only one chance to get your message across to a potential client or associate. Your story must be expressed as professionally and confidently as you can. For most of us who aren't natural-born public speakers that requires some practice. Practicing your story doesn't make it any less yours, but it will help you keep it short and well told.

Here's a step-by-step plan for organizing your own story in an understandable way. Let's use my 30- second story as an example:

Step 1: Describe what was happening before your introduction to the product. Perhaps you want to express some pain that you wanted to relieve, or some want, need or desire you were seeking.

"In February 2006, I was in the advertising business living in NYC. I was feeling bloated, chunky and lethargic. I was overwhelmed with a $2700 rent for a 700 square apartment. I was BBB - busy but broke. I was desperately looking for a better way - when a friend came into the office down 40 pounds and 8 inches off his waist. He was using a nutritional cleansing system and product he had heard about. I was never interested in weight loss as a product or as a business, but I was intrigued by the concept of cleansing."

Step 2: Describe your introduction to the product.

"After I tried the nutritional program, my chiropractor noticed that I was adjusting much more easily than usual. When I told him about this cleansing product, he did the same program and lost 12 pounds. My father went on the program and lost 56 pounds. My energy went through the roof and I dropped down to my high school weight.. So then I went to work. "

Step 3: Describe what has happened since your introduction to the product. This should sound somewhat celebratory!

"Within ten months I replaced my working income, and within the next ten months I turned my monthly income into my weekly income. By the end of that year, my wife, Corey, left her full-time job in corporate real estate, and we love the journey to health, wellness, and financial freedom we are experiencing."

I've told this story hundreds of times over the last few years. It never gets old. People are interested in hearing it because it isn't a canned sales pitch. I may tailor some of the details based on the person or group of people I am talking to, but the format itself is pretty much the same.

Your story is even more valuable than mine – because it is *your* story and it deserves the same type of attention. By perfecting it you will gain the confidence and professionalism necessary to attract the type of people that will help you build your business.

Here's a good formula to follow:

Before (name of company, type of product, benefit of service) I was feeling _____,_____ and _____. Now ever since my friend introduced me to (name of company, type of product, benefit of service)

I fell _____, _____, and _____ . Now I believe people should be able to (benefit of company, product or service)

It looks like this

Before I started JUICITY JUICE I was feeling tired, sluggish and bloated. Ever since my friend introduced me to exotic grape seed from the himalayas I started feeling more energy, more mental clarity and I've been sleeping better. Now I believe mom's can take ownership of their life by eating healthy, and having not only enough energy to run their family but also to have time for themselves.

Please do not read on unless you understand how powerful this is. Yes, it is simple, but it is also profound.

Remember, your product and your compensation plan work. Those are facts. Facts *tell*. Stories *sell*! You will get a lot less resistance from prospective associates when you share your story from your heart rather than when you try to convince people how great your business opportunity is.

Just remember this, you can practice a lot – and you should, but you can't say the right thing to the wrong person or the wrong thing to the right person.

Here's a tip – practice your story in front of a mirror. Make direct eye contact. You will be your toughest critic! If you can do it in front of a mirror – you can do it anywhere!

CHAPTER 8

PROMISES WORTH MAKING AND KEEPING

You're in business for yourself (but not by yourself, remember, you have a team to help you!). You've taken the plunge. You've availed yourself of all the research, you have unshakeable faith in your product, you've perfected the eight step plan and the telling of your 30-second story, and now you're ready to make some serious money and help others to do the same. Before you conquer the world, consider carefully what you are going to present to your potential clients and associates and, more specifically, what you will promise them!

Most of us know "a line" when we hear it. Internet pop-up ads and spam mailboxes are full of them: Make $24,000 in 24 hours while doing nothing from home. Most thinking individuals pass over these ads because they see them for what they are: scams.

The primary way you will separate you from the scam artists, and thereby get a listening to of your product or business, is to take extreme care in what you promise. I can think of two general principles to guide you. There may be others:

1. Do Not Guarantee Vast Sums Of "Easy Money."

Your potential clients or associates have been programmed to believe that opportunities that sound too good to be true usually are. The secret, then, is to present an opportunity that has unlimited potential in extremely realistic terms.

Read that last sentence again carefully. The secret is to present an opportunity that has unlimited potential in extremely realistic terms. It is "the secret" because so few people do it this way.

To put it another way, even though you think your business is unbelievable and incredible, when you are sharing the opportunity make it sound believable and credible.

The sport of golf offers a perspective on this point. Many men and women play golf. The ratio of those who play golf for fun (relatively speaking) to those who play professionally is huge – maybe 100,000 to one. Obviously, not every person who plays golf is going to make a living at it.

Even though you might be a "star associate" or "executive" within your company, the hard work you have put in to attain that status is proof that not everyone else may achieve what you achieve.... and that's fine!

Of course, in an ideal world everyone in your downline would make millions of dollars and make you super-rich, but your goal is to bring people on board with your vision gradually (I'll discuss this at greater length in a future chapter). Instead of beginning the conversation with "Hey, I've got a foolproof way that we can be millionaires and retire early," why not ask simply, "Could you use an extra $500-$1000 every month?" Your prospects will be more inclined to listen to your opportunity and make a fully informed decision.

This is good language to study when handling objections. When people claim that they cannot afford your product or opportunity, you can say something like this:

"Listen, I know times are tough, but let's be honest. If I can help you make just an extra couple of hundred dollars a month, that would help a little bit, right?" (Nodding your head up and down)

As you work with your associates to build their businesses (and yours!) you will develop the type of relationship with them that will make it comfortable and appropriate to dream together about the future; bigger profits and early retirement. Prospects will always respond better to an opportunity that will meet a need, rather than fulfill an outrageous fantasy.

2. MOTIVATORS: PAIN AND PLEASURE

From my experience, there are 2 motivators – pain and pleasure. I have found that most people are more motivated by pain. If you can solve a problem for them, they are likely to join you no matter what you are doing, selling, or promoting. If you can help them with a need, want or desire, they will go along with you. In this economy, if you can help people make an extra $200 a week – even an extra $200 a month – you would be helping a lot of people.

If you want to get rich – or at least make a lot of money in this profession

– you will have to help a lot of people make some extra money. The more people you help, the more money you make. The more problems you solve for people, the more successful you will be.

Here's a tip: The answer is always in the question. When people ask, "how much money will I make?" – a good answer is "how much work are you willing to put in?", or "will you guarantee my success?" Perhaps you would respond, "Will you guarantee me your work ethic?"

The dance between pain and pleasure is often finicky. There is a story of a dog who sits down on the porch and starts to cry. The man is sitting in his rocking chair reading the paper. The dog continues to cry.

The neighbor comes over and asks, "why the dog is crying"?

The man responds, "'because he is sitting on a nail"

"Why doesn't he just get up?" the man asks.

"Because he is not in enough pain"

So when you are out and about, remember that people are motivated by pain and pleasure. However, most people are comfortably numb. They have cell phones, microwaves and clean water, and if they do - they are in the top 1% wealthiest people in the world. There are a lot of people who are in so much pain - they hate their job or their boss of their commute. They work so hard but can't get ahead. They are in just enough pain to be bored, or to complain but not in enough pain to do anything about it. On the other hand, there are people with big dreams. They want more out of life. They want to travel the world, play golf or sail or visit foreign cities or beautiful beaches. But the pleasure they seek eludes them. It is mere fantasy. The stick is too long and the carrot is too small. So they don't do what it takes to achieve their dreams. That's why you often hear people in our profession talking about "finding your why" and "make your why so big you cry"

Your job is to identify this pain or the pleasure and then off your product or service as a solution. When I was introduced to Network Marketing almost 20 years ago, I was in the right amount of pain and had my sites on a bigger pleasure and purpose. Remember you can't say the wrong thing to the right person and the right thing to the wrong person.

You offer your program as a solution to someone who is in a lot of pain and will do anything to get out of it, or a person who is so clear on their big vision and purpose. I know a woman who was in so much pain that she sold her refrigerator to get started. Eighteen months later she was at 6 figures a year. This is certainly not the norm. She busted her butt, she was coachable, she followed the system and had a relentless work ethic. I know another woman who adopted and fostered 12 children. They were practically on food stamps when they started and Network Marketing was the only vehicle they could find to fund their lifestyle. They were mission driven for sure. I'm not recommending you prospect people on food stamps. You will be best served prospecting the most successful people you know. I tend to look for professionals or people who have had success in some area of their life.

I used to tell people they could replace their income with Network Marketing. Now I tell people they can create some extra weekly cash flow. When I first started I would tell people they could create a 6 figure business from the comfort of their home. Now I tell people that could create an income part time on the side that could cover a car payment or a house payment. Back in the day I would tell people they could double or triple their income. Now I tell people they if they work hard and follow a system, if they plug into our structure and they are coachable, they can potentially add 10-20% to their income. In other words, keeping it real. I said before this business can be incredible and unbelievable. Some buy into that. You will have more success making sound credible and believable.

CHAPTER 9

THE GRADIENT

———————

Healthy relationships are defined by successive positive interactions between two people over the course of a period of time. We tend not to share the intimate details of our lives with strangers or even casual acquaintances. At the same time, we are especially wary of those who would share those details with us after meeting us for the first or second time.

Question: What's easier to walk on – a gently sloping ground or a steep hill?

The lower the slope, the easier it is to get to your destination. If the destination you want people to get to is joining your business, don't give them a mountain of information to climb.

When a business places a ramp outside of it's building to assist the wheelchair bound customers, state law or local ordinance defines the ramp's maximum degree of slope. That's because if the slope – or gradient

» is too steep, people who need it will not be able to use it. You want to use this same principle of gradient in presenting your opportunity and building your business.

STEP 1: TURN EVERYDAY ENCOUNTERS INTO OPPORTUNITIES TO SHARE YOUR 30- SECOND STORY.

For you, as a business builder, the proper answer to "How are you?" is always "Great" or "Super" or "Fantastic" with a great big smile on your face. Sometimes when I am feeling super silly I will say, "I am amazing, but I am getting better!"

Undoubtedly, your contacts have asked the same question dozens of times and received the pat answer. They will be intrigued by an upbeat response, which will lead to the sharing of the reason you're happy – your 30-second story.

In fact, when most people say, "How are you?", they don't even wait for an answer most of the time. So how do you turn everyday acquaintances into life-long friends and potential business partners?

How about this dialogue?

Them: How are you? You: I'M CELEBRATING!! Them: What are you celebrating?

Now you give your 30-second story!

STEP 2: MAINTAIN A COMFORTABLE RATIO OF WHAT YOU OFFER AND WHAT YOU DEMAND.

Remember, building your business depends on your prospect's level of interest, so consider the prospecting business as a sort of courtship. A man smitten with affection for a woman will shower her with gifts, nice dinners, and expressions of love. As the relationship matures and love begins to deepen, the man will decide to ask for the lady's hand in marriage – when the time is right. A man intuitively understands the consequences when the question of marriage is brought up too quickly.

So it is with your business opportunity. Offer value to your prospects at the commencement of your relationship. Become genuinely interested in their lives – especially if they have already have a business or a line of work they are happy in. When they become dissatisfied with their affairs, chances are they will seek you out.

A good way to practice this is with questions such as:

"How are you?"	"How are you doing?"
"How can I help you?"	"What are you looking for?"
"How long have you been at this job?"	"What do you do when you are not working?"
"What do you like most about your job?"	"What do you like least?"
*"How long have you been working here?"	*"Are you going to work here another (insert time)?"

I love this combination of questions.

me: "So, what do you do?"

them: "I'm a ... fill in the blank (nurse, a teacher, an accountant)"

me: "Wow. That's cool. How long have you been doing that?"

them "Three years."

me "are you going to do it another three years?"

People will answer this last question with something like "not if I can help it" or "unless I win the lottery" or "I hope not" or sometimes they will say "yes of course, I love it"

Then, I respond with:

"Do you keep your options open for additional streams of income?" or "If you didn't work here, what would you rather be doing"?

The goal is to create dialogue.

Sometimes I will say, "Wow! You've been here 3 years you must love it." or "Three years - that's incredible... you seem pretty sharp and talented, they must pay you pretty well."

Often these types of questions will get people opening up to you. Once you get good at identifying a pain or a want or a desire ... and offering a solution, you will start to attract your perfect customer and business partner.

As you learn these strategies, and you practice them, you will get better and better at creating conversations. If this sounds basic to you, then start teaching this to your team. You will be surprised at how new this material is to them. If you are finding this languaging to be helpful, then practice it. Every master was once a disaster. These phrases take a minute to learn and a lifetime to master. They work with warm market and cold market.

First we learn what to do and say to our warm market, the people we know. Then we learn what to do and say to people in our cold market, people we meet. Eventually we learn what to do and say to attract people to you. This is the law of attraction in action. I can assist you with all of it .. make sure to visit www.drewberman.com often for tips, techniques and strategies.

STEP 3: TO BUILD FOR THE LONG-TERM, FIND PEOPLE WITH A LONG-TERM ATTITUDE.

There are people in the world who are looking for the easy million-dollar check. They are the people who point and click on every get-rich-quick scheme on the Internet and they are not the type of people you want to invest in.

The best network marketers understand this. If you recruit someone with a "hard sell" approach, or by promising them outrageous fame and fortune in a short period of time, they may join you, but these folks will do very little to build your business and may end up quitting within 30 days. Why? Because they joined you for the *wrong reasons*!

Too many people approach Network Marketing and forget the first part of the word – *network*. You are building a network of business associates and friends who will buy into your opportunity when the time is right *for them*. When they do join, you want them to stick with the opportunity. Otherwise, your time and effort is lost.

Look at the relationship example one more time. This is an example of too steep a gradient:

"Hi, it was fun meeting you tonight at this party. Do you want to get married and have 7 kids with me?"

Here is how it translates to Network Marketing:

"Hi, this is the best opportunity in the world and if you give me $1,000 and sign up for auto-ship and buy a ticket to the national convention and tell all your friends and family that this is the greatest product they have ever seen and you do everything I say and talk to my mentor and coach 2 or 3 times a week then you can actually get rich and financially free and you can fire your boss and travel around the world and never have to work again!!"

Now, do you at least understand what *not* to do? Remember, yes, it is unbelievable and incredible. It is also believable and credible, and I recommend that you present it that way.

Keep it real. Keep it light. Keep it fun. If you are brand new and just learning don't pretend to be an overnight guru. If you are a teacher and you just start your Network Marketing business, don't show up to your friends as an expert in marketing or nutrition or whatever the benefits of your program are. If people know you as an engineer don't show up at the party telling people you are expanding your international company helping people save money by shopping on line.

Be honest. "I'm a teacher, but I just started this program on the side that is helping people lose weight the new way. I'm excited to try this program that has worked for my friend, want to do it with me?" Or, "I am an engineer full time, but part time on the side I have an ecommerce business that helps people like us save more on their electric bill, it's fun and could be lucrative, would you be open to hearing more?"

I remember back in high school football, we always went over the basics. Even right before the playoffs we would focus on blocking and tackling. Blocking and tackling. Blocking and tackling. Same thing with Network Marketing. Learn and master the basics. Then teach it over and over. Teach people how to connect. Assist people on their marketing and outreach. Work with your team on how to create conversations. As you learn, implement. As you implement, teach. As you teach, duplicate.

Duplication is key. Treat this like a franchise. If you attract people who are generally looking for an opportunity, then you can use this example - "Imagine investing in a franchise like a McDonalds or a Subway or a Dunkin Donuts. They could cost $500,000 - $1,000,000. Well our program is very similar. Except it doesn't cost a million or even half a million. It doesn't cost a 100 grand or even 50 grand. In fact it has all the upside potential of a traditional franchise without all the risk. It doesn't cost $20,000 or even $10,000 or even $5,000. For a lot less then $2,000 you get a business that is not limited to a storefront, your zip code or even your country. You have a limitless internet based business that could provide you with the lifestyle that most only dream of. Some earn a car payment by working this part time on the side. Others share the products and opportunity passively, but with focus and can earn a rent payment or a mortgage payment. Wouldn't it be cool if we can make your biggest monthly payment disappear? Now some take this a little more seriously and build it to 5 grand or 10 grand a month and some are able to create a nice retirement income."

How does the above script sound to you? Incredible and unbelievable, or credible and believable. What would happen if you practiced that in the mirror … I bet you'd get better. Most people fall in love with their product or service, but they are not taught how to talk about the business. Most who are taught exactly what to say still don't. This business is made up of mostly customers and once in a while sharers. About 80% of the people in Network Marketing never refer anyone. Never. Not one. Even if they say they want to, they don't know what to say. Or they don't know who to say it to. Or, they don't know how to say it. The folks in the 80% are happy to make 0-$500 a month. They like the product, the culture, the team work, the support, the events, the fun and the community. Serve them. Love them. Acknowledge them. Recognize them. They make up a bulk of your business. These are your customers. Don't ask how can I retain my people. Ask how can I love and acknowledge and recognize my people better and more often so that they love sticking around. This is company and team culture.

Out of the remaining 20%, most will be happy if they can make $500-$2000 per month. Don't pressure them to do more. Love them where they are at. Encourage them. Help them.

A very, very small percentage of people who join Network Marketing have the interest, time, talent, skills, habits, mindset, patience, and where-with-all to earn more the 2 grand a month. Even if they show up at every event, they are on every phone call and swear they will be your next big star. It just ain't so. The cool part about it is you probably see yourself in one of the percentages above. Awareness is the first step. You can grow yourself and your skills. You can change. I believe in you. And I can help you get from where you are to where you want to go.

Chapter 10

THE KEY TO FOLLOW UP

———

Many well-meaning people who embark on the journey to success in Network Marketing often find themselves making an unscheduled stop in a vast, uncharted wasteland. A minute spent there is a minute wasted. Several hours or days spent there can cripple a business and stunt its growth.

What is the name of this vast wasteland? MaybeLand. Once you start recruiting associates it is absolutely essential to steer your ship away from it. A well-planned follow up strategy will help.

The primary way to avoid this wasteland is to remind yourself how valuable your time is. If you were to take the yearly income of the most successful business people in the world to determine how much their time was worth, you compute an hourly rate of several *thousand* dollars per hour!

Your time is no less valuable and the word "maybe" coming from a prospective associate robs you of that time. You want your prospects to give you a definite "yes" or "no." Take a moment right now and ask yourself, how much am I worth an hour? Literally.

What number did you come up with? Why? What did you base it on? Did you base it on how much you think you are worth? Did you base it on how much you would pay someone else to do what you do? Are you basing it on your pre-Network Marketing business? Are you basing it on your current level in your Network Marketing business? Or are you basing it on where you would like to be in your Network Marketing business? Or, you may be stating how much you are making now hourly.

Would you like to know what my number is? $1,000. That's right – a thousand bucks an hour. Would you like to know how I came up with that number? I figured I got into this business not to make $100,000 a year; I got into this business for $100,000 a month! Why? Because that's what the millionaires I have learned from have said is possible that I can make.

So I took the path of the millionaire from the beginning story, rather than the mindset of the accountant.

I believe. I actually believe that I will not only be a millionaire in this profession, but I can actually make a million dollars a year in this profession. If other people can do it, then I can do it, right? If I can do it than you can do it, right?

So where does $1,000 an hour come from? Well if I make $100,000 a month, that's $25,000 a week. I think I can handle 25 hours a week of work, that's $1,000 an hour. Hmm! Now I know that might be not a lot of money to live on – especially because I live in Fairfield County – but it is a good start!

HERE'S HOW I NAVIGATE AWAY FROM MAYBELAND.

1. I build a relationship with my prospective associates and look for opportunities to share my 30- second story. My approach might change depending on whom I am speaking with, but the key is

the same: building a relationship based on common ground or common experiences.

2. I ask one or more of the following questions: "If I could show you a way to make an extra $500-$1000 a month, would that help you or be of interest to you?"

"How's business in this shaky economy?

"Would you look at a gold mine if it were lucrative, part time, and could fit into your schedule?"

3. Our company has an 8-minute video online. I ask them to view it and set up a phone appointment in one or two days. Setting up the appointment is key. If you are not setting appointments you are missing out on probably 75% of your follow-ups. It's so important, I want you to repeat it to yourself right now: setting up the appointment is key (remember step 3?).

Most people in our profession will meet a contact and say something like, "watch this video and let's talk in a couple of days and you can tell me what you think. " Then they will put that name and number on their eternal "never-closing-never-ending-continuous-can't- get-them-on-the-phone-leave-a-ton-of-messages-   pain-in-the-butt-pretend-non-existent" follow-up list.

I will say something like this:

"It was great to meet you. You have great energy and can make a ton of money in my profession. Because you impressed me, I will give you access to some information that can help you add 20, maybe 30%, to your income. We are putting together a team that I think you will be a great asset to. Watch this video."

(This is a verbal command. Polite. No begging involved—just do it. Why? Because we have rapport, because I told you to, and because it will benefit you.)

"When is usually best to connect mornings or afternoons?

Afternoon? Great."

"What's better – tomorrow or Thursday? Tomorrow?"

"Ok I have 1:15 free or I can do 3:45. 3:45? Perfect – I will call you then."

"Which is the best number to reach you at? Ok, and what is a backup number just in case?"

"OK, perfect – and give me your email so I can shoot you out that info. Cool – talk to you tomorrow at 3:45!"

Later, I will e-mail them when I am in front of my computer to confirm –same tone, similar conversation, confirmation of the video, and the time. If you don't set up definite time to speak with your prospect it then becomes almost impossible to track them down, which sets you up for a trip to MaybeLand. I like to follow through, rather than just to follow up.

4. During the initial phone appointment, I answer any questions they might have about the opportunity; usually I allow a maximum of two questions. That's right – two (2) questions. Then I will start asking the questions. I might then ask them one of the following:

"It comes with 100% money back guarantee. Have I given you enough information to just at least give it a shot?"

"After viewing the video, how do you see the product working for you? Better health, better wealth, or both?"

One of my favorite questions to ask a prospect is:

"Now that you have seen the video presentation, how would you like to see our company benefit you and help you in your life?"

Sit back, read that again, and take it in. That question – worded exactly that way – will make you a lot of money. You will do a lot less convincing and selling. They will be selling you on why you should work with them. This, my friend, is called "posture"!

Now you do not have to decide if they want the product or the business opportunity. They will tell you! The answer is always YES.

When I heard that sentence – that's right, I heard that sentence from Leann Jackson at a seminar – I knew – I *knew* – it would make me thousands of dollars. It has, and it can for you, too.

5. From that point, if your prospect is ready to join, you might set up a three-way call with your team leader or invite them to one of your company's events in the area.

   Three-way calls, in my opinion, are one of the best tools in our whole profession. You get to use a product and/or business opportunity expert, for free, to explain the process and answer any questions.

   Wow! When I learned to master that everything exploded. Everything.

   I knew I could introduce people to other people. That is easy – let them do the talking. Done deal.

   Whatever your course, make sure that your prospect is confident of your support so that he or she does not become discouraged.

   None of the steps I have mentioned above need to be completed in any particular order. I base these steps on the "gradient" principle

I discussed earlier, as well as my own experiences in my company. However, *the key to effective follow up is following through.*

Bring each of your prospects to a conclusion that removes all doubts and keeps you far away from MaybeLand.

Here are some other prospecting nuggets: I like to say:

"On a scale from 1 to 10, 10 being you are ready to start right now, 1 being 'do not ever bring this up again', where are you?"

If they said a 6, I would ask: "How I can help you get to an 8?"

I would never ask "how do I get you to a 10?" That would be too steep a gradient. I would then handle their objections and move forward.

Lately, I have been trying something new. Remember, I try new things as I learn them, too. I'm still a student who happens to be mentoring other students!

If they say 4, I say: "Why so high?"

When I heard Jack Canfield say that I nearly choked. Brilliant! I have tried that lately and generally get people telling me all the things they like about me and my company and my opportunity!

When I am feeling really bold I will say: "On a scale of yes to no, where are you?"

Ok, let's apply what we've learned here. On a separate sheet of Paper, draw a staircase. On the top step, I want you to write down what you want to achieve by getting involved in Network Marketing. Be specific. Don't just write down 'financial freedom'. Write down exactly what you will do once you are financially free!

On the bottom step, I want you to write the first key concept we learned for finding and keeping associates: Build Rapport.

What you write on the other steps is up to you. Use what you've learned here. Talk to your team members, your mentor and your coach. Get their input. Come up with a solid plan for achieving your dreams. Then, keep in front of your computer and look at it often. Remind yourself where you are and where you are going.

Chapter 11

BE THE CHANGE YOU WANT TO SEE

I mentioned earlier that the only person holding you back from fulfilling all of your dreams and goals is you. I want to share a thought with you:

Insanity, as defined by Albert Einstein, is doing the same actions over and over again and expecting a different result. Whether you are an executive or just starting out in your field you will come to the point where the growth of your business slows down and the "flow" seems to have stopped. When you come to these times in your career, if you continue doing what you have always done, you will go crazy. It's like beating your head against a wall and expecting it not to hurt.

If you humbly admit that you might need to improve your system or practices and seek out a different approach to your opportunity you give yourself the chance to take your business to a higher level. If you continue to be a student, your potential for success increases.

If you attract consumers, then your business will grow linearly. If you attract other networkers, your business will grow exponentially. One dedicated, experienced network marketer is worth 1,000 consumers.

Celebrate your successes where they come, but don't be afraid to push yourself and your business.

Learn to stretch and add more weapons to your arsenal. There is a wealth of knowledge out there and much of it is free to anyone with an Internet connection. Use it. Study it. Make your business grow!

Take all of your skills, your talents, your faith, your commitment to self-improvement, everything that makes you who you are, and make your vision a reality!

In my opinion, your belief level needs to be high in five areas for you to win in this profession. Rate yourself 1 out of 10, 10 being absolute belief, in each of these areas. If you are less than a 10, you know what you need to work on.

I believe in my product   1 2 3 4 5 6 7 8 9 10

I believe in my company   1 2 3 4 5 6 7 8 9 10

I believe in my support team   1 2 3 4 5 6 7 8 9 10

I believe in the profession   1 2 3 4 5 6 7 8 9 10

I believe in myself   1 2 3 4 5 6 7 8 9 10

and lastly

I believe in myself,

in Network Marketing   1 2 3 4 5 6 7 8 9 10

I hope I gave you some nuggets that you can use, implement and teach. Network Marketing can be an expensive hobby, or if can be a lucrative business. It is not a get rich quick scheme, although some are able to make fast money. It is a business that takes skills, confidence, mindset, training and practice. It can be frustrating at times. It has good seasons and bad seasons. People who seem to rise to the top quickly and others who take years. Over time you will want to learn team building, prospecting and recruiting, customer service, networking, and marketing. You will be challenged. You will have good times and bad times. You will constantly need to work on your belief, and your desire. I believe in you, more than you will ever know. And I'm here to help.

Chapter 12

YOU ONLINE/YOU OFFLINE

Our business is going through a significant shift. Shift happens! We all need to be ahead of the curve. In order to thrive in our business, we need to understand the past, present and future of Network Marketing.

The profession of Network Marketing has matured through the years and it is now ready for the biggest breakthrough in its history.

The past is past, we can learn from it of course, but we always need to be grounded in the basics. The basics of Network Marketing are simply P+P=P; people + product = profit. It's the same with any profession. Same with Nike. Same with AT&T. Same with Pepsi. Network Marketing is about serving people with an amazing line of products, while generating income for ourselves and our families. The more people that buy into our product, the more profit for us. That's it. Period.

The present state of our profession is somewhat confusing and a bit uncertain. Where does the Internet fit in exactly? What game are you playing? Are you a network marketer learning to market online? Are you an Internet marketer trying to learn the basics of Network Marketing? There is a lot to talk about and to evaluate. Some of you have no interest in online activities and have no idea what marketing is. Some of your teammates think that *they are* the company, they are the product, and their Facebook picture (their Facebook avatar) is a picture of their super juice of the month. Wrong

When building an online and offline business, and when striving to combine the two, we have to address who *you are*, and who *you are being*, both online and offline. Your company will certainly have a way that they market, with some restrictions on what you can do online. Some of your teammates are only using their corporate replicated website (yourname. company.com).

However, things are changing and they are changing fast. For many years people will continue to market the traditional way, or showcase their products or opportunity this way. There is a big difference when moving online. One needs to understand the essence of marketing to be successful at both. What it means to showcase your product or opportunity in a way that attracts people to you; people who already have a need for your product, idea or service. For instance, Facebook is a social platform; you should have pictures of your family, your kids, you doing fun stuff. It's not the place to always be selling. Connecting yes, selling no. We do have some creative ways to attract people to us for sure. It's an art, not an exact science.

The future of our profession is changing dramatically. The Internet is still fairly new when compared to how long business has been around. Facebook is here to stay, until something better comes along. Personal branding is key, for some, a foreign concept to others. I didn't start personal branding until I was at 5 figures a month.. This concept will get more and more important as the years go by. People will want to know all about you, why they should join up with you, and how you can help them. There will always be some people who lead with their product and there will always be some who lead with the opportunity. There will be many who fail, but there will be many more who succeed now, thanks to branding online.

Fortunes are going to be made, online and offline, in the next few years. There is an unprecedented wave of change coming our way. I am sure that you have heard this before: there are three types of people; those who make things happen, those who watch things happen, and those who wonder, "Hey, what happened?" Which group do you want to be in?

I can't possibly teach you all there is to know about being online in this book. Things are changing daily. If I told you everything that I know it would bore some of you and excite others. I can rattle off the importance of having a blog, having a presence on Facebook, the difference between a group page and a fan page, how to generate leads on Linkedin, what the best pay strategies are and the best free strategies, or what are the best keywords and how to find them. Then there is how to use your corporate site and what other systems are out there to use and how. What a Squidoo 'lens' is and how to use HootSuite, PPC vs PPV and when to market what, and what to market when. Everything I know and use, learned through trial and error, is at www.drewberman.com. Join me there.

You now have wings, my friend. The roots of Network Marketing run deep and this profession is *the* one to watch. We are attracting athletes, doctors, stay-at- home moms, millionaires, real estate agents, authors, speakers, 20-somethings and baby boomers. Some of you prefer to pick up the phone and call people while others like to meet belly-to-belly. If you don't show some of your teammates, current and future, how to master the basics - connect with people, make appointments, show presentation, follow up - then you will not succeed.

For those of you who do not know what Google+ is, or how to use Google Analytics, or what the heck Market Samurai is, don't worry. You can't learn it all in a day, and you may never catch up with all of it, which is OK as well. I recommend the Learn and Earn program. We can help you navigate through these waters.

Keep learning, keep earning! This is the key to this whole book. This point is going to be relevant and timely for the immediate future of Network Marketing and, in my opinion, will separate the people who do well and those who do great. Those who catch the wave and learn how to market themselves online *and* offline are the ones who will make it big.

For those of you who stay offline, old school, the times they are a-changin'! It's time to plug in, understand when and how to automate things online. Learn how to generate online leads. For the online marketers out there, the 20-somethings out of school who have never used a payphone, and the experts on data capture pages who have lead generation systems out the wazoo, but get nauseous with the thought of building a business by actually being *on the phone with people* - YUCK... just shoot me! I think you are in for a rude awakening.

Network Marketing is the way of the future, my friend, whether you choose to build online or offline or both. The essence of who are you *being*, is most important. Who are you? Once you are clear about this and your message stays consistent, whether at a Chamber of Commerce event, or when you are connecting with someone on the latest and greatest social media platform, you will be most successful. You want to be *you*; brand yourself, not your company.

Make connections with real people, whether it be at a BNI morning breakfast opportunity meeting, or when you are connecting with someone from your new connection app on your cell phone.

The network marketers who are going to create long- term, passive and residual income, are the ones who have more leads then they have time. They have learned how to talk to their warm market, how to meet people when they are out and about, and then how to turn them into leads, in that order. The ones who can do that, and teach it, are the ones who are going to win, and win big in Network Marketing.

So, I leave you with this. Congratulations on your Commencement. The college graduation, the ending of school, the commencement, is the beginning of life and pursuit of a career. The end of this book brings the beginning of your learning. We are committed to bringing the best of the best of online and offline marketing techniques, what's working now, and future predictions at www.drewberman.com.

The Internet is the new frontier, but don't get lost in cyberspace, you still have to pick up the/ phone. The easiest place to start online with minimal barriers, even for the technophobes, is Facebook. Once you have an account, make some friends; join some groups, just like you would offline. Then look into a fan page and maybe form a group. A good goal is to connect with 50 friends, then 500 friends, then 5000 friends. Post interesting thoughts that express who you are. Eventually, you might look into a Pay-Per-Click (PPC) campaign.... When you are ready, I can assist you with that.

Stay excited, stay committed, stay informed, stay in the game! It is your future we are talking about and you now have great tools to take you to new heights in your business - online and offline. See you up there!

2020 HINDSIGHT OR 2020 FORESIGHT?

The year 2020 is right around the corner. In 2020, how old will you be? What will your relationships be like? How about your income?

Hobbies? Ultimately ... what will be your 2020 lifestyle?

If you are lucky enough to be reading this before the year 2020, great: We have some planning to do. If you are reading this post-2020, then you have 2020 hindsight, as the saying goes, and you can use these principles for 1, 3, 5 years out. The goal and purpose is to assist you with living in prepare, rather than in repair. If we work together, we can live in preparation for the life we want to live, which is a better choice than repairing how we used to live.

The good news is that wherever you are, whatever you do, you are reading this now. And now is the best time to start. Start what? Creating the life you want, not living the life you don't want. You are familiar with the Law of Attraction, right? If not, that would be a good place to start. What does living a life by design mean to you? What is the good life?

For me, it's about lifestyle. Lifestyle is vague enough to allow you to give it the appropriate meaning. It's also specific enough to realize we all want a better lifestyle. How we define it is up to each individual, of course. "Lifestyle" can mean many things to many people, but it usually includes some basic life pleasures and/or necessities from a variety of topics. It is of course a wide range, but the basics include a similar theme for most people. Most of us, from janitor to CEO, from jail to Yale, want a better lifestyle.

We want to worship the way we wish, as often as we like, wherever we want. We probably want more time with friends and family. Most people want to be in contribution of some sort. It's important to have good health, right? Making money is important too, isn't it? Typically this means not necessarily being rich, per se, but having enough funds to enjoy ourselves—or at least pay the bills. For the most part, more money will help. Some of us want to pursue more hobbies. Golf is an all-day event, and so is skiing. These activities need time.

Being loved, being involved in worthwhile projects, having fun are some other needs.

Wherever you go around the country, or around the world, most people want a better lifestyle. Most people, however, have a JOB, and most JOBs are determined by the employer. Most JOBS are paid what the job is worth, not what the person is worth. I think it's safe to say that most people don't love their job. Do you? If you do, congratulations—you are one of the lucky ones. If you don't, congratulations again—you are normal. In fact, whether you like your job or not, would you like the ability to earn 10% more next year? How about 20% more? Would making an addition 20% from what you made last year improve your life by 20%? Or more?

For most people, a 20% increase in income would dramatically improve their lifestyle.

So what would it take for you dramatically improve your lifestyle? Here's the good news, friends: There is a way. We are moving to a production-based society. Technology and the international market place are making it harder and harder to a) maintain our current lifestyle, b) improve our current lifestyle c) make more money d) have more free time. There is a solution, and this solution is becoming more and more prevalent in society.

In the US there are two major tax systems. (There are actually many, but predominantly two.) The first one is for the EMPLOYEE. This is a person who usually has a JOB and a BOSS and A DESK. This tax form is called W2. On a W2 tax form, one is paid, then the government takes its share, and then one is expected to pay their expenses with whatever is left over. This in essence is a huge tax disadvantage, and not generally consistent with the employee's best interest. The IRS wins big time in this scenario.

The other major tax form in the US is called a 1099. This is for the Entrepreneur. In this situation one gets paid, and then pays their expenses, and then the government takes their share. In fact, the computer I am typing this on was a tax deduction, meaning I paid for it, deducted it from my income, and then paid taxes on the remaining income.

Wow! This is also true for my office, my cell phone, my car, most dinners out, most of my trips including hotel and air, and many other tax benefits.

But isn't being an entrepreneur risky? Not any more, especially with downsizing, corporate shifting, relocating, outsourcing, and other creative ways that corporations are using to get rid of their biggest expense, which of course, is employees. Yup, that's right. I said it: If you are an employee, you are an expense. You are paid the least amount so that you will not quit, and you probably work as little as possible not to be fired. This situation applies not necessarily to you, but most probably to someone you know.

If you have a JOB that gives you the lifestyle you want, that allows you to live with passion and purpose, if you are often heard saying TGIM (Thank God it's Monday) because you are so enthusiastic about starting the week, contributing to people's lives, and living a lifestyle by design ... then congratulations ... but you are in the minority.

If most people want to FIRE their BOSS and/or they want a 20% or more raise and/or they want a better lifestyle and/or find that their JOB is getting in the way of their life—then THERE IS A SOLUTION. THERE IS A BETTER WAY.

Every day that goes by that you do not have a home-based business, you are throwing money out the window. With a home-based business, whether you are a 5-figure yearly earner, a 6-figure yearly earner, or a 7-figure yearly earner, a home-based business can give you:

»   extra weekly income

»   a retirement plan

»   huge tax advantages

»   flexibility

»   10%-20% or more increase in your current income (or more)

»   a support team

»   no boss

»   no commute

»   no begging for raises

»   and a better lifestyle.

Consider that part about a better lifestyle and what it may mean to different individuals. I've broken this concept into three parts. Picture a triangle, and in the middle, write the words My Ideal Lifestyle.

It you we are talking about now. On one side of the triangle, write the words Better Health. On the next side, write the words Better Wealth.

And on the third side, write the words More Time Freedom. Improvement in each of these areas will generally improve one's lifestyle.

Now, what if you are able to achieve only two of these. Well, let's see. Let's look at these scenarios. You have great abundant health and a ton of free time ... but you are broke.

In this situation, you might not have the best lifestyle. Let's look at someone with a ton of free time and oodles of money, but terrible health. Not the best lifestyle, right?

What's the third option? Lots and lots of money, great health, and no time to enjoy it (this one might describe most people who have become slaves to the dollar or the boss or the job.)

Guess what: You can actually have all three. You can have better health, better wealth and more free time—if you take care of yourself, focus on the things that keep you happy, and have passive/residual income.

Most people have active, non-residual income: If they go to work, they get paid. If they don't go to work, they don't get paid. Most people get paid by the hour, by the client, by the project, etc. This is linear. With a home-based business, you can have exponential income. Some who get engaged can make a car payment or a house payment; some can increase their income by 10%, some by 20%—and some can double or even triple their income.

I teach people how to go from hobby income to professional income with a home-based business.

If you are looking for a better way, there is a solution. Many have been able to improve their health, increase their income, and, have more free time. How? With the proper home-based business, you can leverage yourself. You can work with others.

You can have income coming in from multiple sources. We've developed systems to follow and a structure for success—structure and flexibility. You can start a home-based business part time on the side or go full time right away.

Isn't there a huge investment? Not anymore.

If you or someone you know wants to learn about the ins and outs, wants a free tip or two, or is ready to start a home-based business, please reach out: We might be able to assist you as we have many in the past.

2020 hindsight: I woulda coulda shoulda. 2020 foresight: Let's create that lifestyle by design.

I have had a home-based business for over 15 years. I get to spend a lot of time with my family, don't have to deal with long commutes, and I can create a lifestyle by design. My team and I can help you create your lifestyle by design. We can help you achieve better health, better wealth and more free time. Give us a call. Let's see if we can work together to help you achieve your goals. Call us at 800-517-3220 or visit us online at www.drewberman.com

If you found this book to be valuable, please refer your teams to www.drewberman.com There you will find constant updates and cutting edge material on the Network Marketing community and profession..

Stay tuned for audio training, workbooks, video training, one-on-one coaching, group coaching, summits and other great tools to help you reach your goals in Network Marketing.

I am currently available for one-on-one and group coaching. Our programs run from 3 months to a year, and different curriculums are available for all budgets. I have had the honor and pleasure of working with people brand new, and seasoned experts. I've assisted folks in their first company and in their 18th company. Our tips and techniques have worked with some of the best of the best in the world. In addition to Network Marketing I am a Certified Extreme Focus Coach. We use patented techniques and modalities that work with elite athletes in MLB, NCAA, NFL, and the Olympics. They have been used with Army Rangers, Navy Seals and The US Pentagon. In other words, they work. For my high end clients, we have retreats and masterminds sometimes at Spring Training in Arizona, with the Army Rangers in Las Vegas, or at the Olympic Training Center in Colorado. These are way cool.

As a Peak Performance Strategist and Life Architect, I help you navigate through the tough waters of operating a successful home based business. Many people who enter our profession end up running a non for profit business from the discomfort of their home. I can assist you with mindset, goals, the law of attraction, marketing, sales, networking, building a brand and time management. We can assist you with your life breakthroughs. We help with structure, accountability and peak performance hacks. And for sure, I can assist you on your Network Marketing journey, no matter where you are.

I can be contacted about coaching at www.drewberman.com

www.DrewBerman.com

DREW'S WORDS OF WISDOM

So, who am I? I am Drew Berman and I live at www.drewberman.com. I have been in sales and marketing for more than 30 years, and Network Marketing for 20 years. I was introduced to Network Marketing in 2001 when I was 29 years old, after I came back from a bicycle ride around the world. I completed a 35-Country Bike Tour in the year 2000 called Odyssey 2000. I had seen the world. I tasted freedom. And I wanted to go from the good life to the great life. After my big trip, I thought Real Estate would be my ticket. I was trying to get back into real estate, trying to figure it all out.

I attended a BNI meeting and I met a man there who introduced me to the Network Marketing profession. He started by developing a rapport, he was creating a relationship, and then he complimented me. He said, "you seemed like a sharp guy. Are you locked into what you're doing or you're open-minded for other streams of income?" He gave me a CD called 'High Tech and High Touch'. The next thing I knew, I was in Amway. I had no idea, because they were rebranding as Quixtar.

So, for five years I chased the dream and the sizzle, but I could never find the steak. I can't say anything bad about the Amway Corporation. They've done great things for this profession. They do billions of dollars in sales a year around the globe. So did some other major NM companies - The Big 5 I call them: Amway, Avon, NuSkin, HerbaLife and Mary Kay.

These are, or were, the giants of the industry.

However, the Baby Boomers remember what it was like when people had garages full of the soap and shampoo and they may be reluctant to join this profession. Now, the twenty-somethings are entering the workforce with no history and with no preconceived notion of this profession.

So how do you talk to both groups? How do you offer Network Marketing to professionals who are used to having a boss, but who are entrepreneurial? Well, this is no secret sauce.

This is why we have created our new website called www.thelawofaffluence.com. *Who are you*? Not so much of *what* are you doing, but *who* are you being. You attract who you are, not who you want to be. Please visit it now to change your future!

If you look on drewberman.com you can see some of the people that I have hung out with. You will see Cynthia Kersey, who wrote the book 'Unstoppable'.

There is a picture of me with Jack Canfield, from the bestselling Chicken Soup series. There is also a picture of me with Deepak Chopra!

So, here is a tip for you when you're out about, whenever you are at events or functions with anyone credible, just get your picture taken with them. This is essential for personal branding. When you get your picture taken with experts, people then assume that you are an expert.

There is a picture of me with Jeffrey Combs. We did two training programs together last year. We shared the stage together and it was awesome. There is a picture of me with Dr. John Gray from "Men are From Mars and Women are from Venus".

John Gray, Jack Canfield and I all work in the same profession and in the same company. We are trainers for a company that is the world leader in nutritional cleansing. We promote an anti-aging and fat-burning system that rids the body of toxins and impurities, releasing excess weight in the process.

John Gray lost nearly 30 pounds with the products. He began to see brain chemistry shifting, with women increasing levels of serotonin and men of dopamine. After seeing this incredible change in people, he became a national trainer. So did I.

You will also see me with Les Brown (perhaps the most popular motivational speaker alive today) and Harv Eker (from Millionaire Mind Intensive). Does this make me great or better? No. What it does mean is that I carry my camera with me when I'm out and about. I know how to connect with folks and that is a wonderful asset.

Here is a good question: how do make someone appear in you life? You make them a PEER in your life. Then people will come to you. You look at people online with all of these marketing systems and blogs and they are just regular people. So, when you meet them, go say, "Hi". Get your picture taken with them, because that's how people are going to remember you, and that's how you'll create a list of professionals and experts.

So, brand yourself, because you are not your company, you are not your product. You are you, and *who you are* is going to change everything for you.

Ten years in Network Marketing and five years in Amway. I couldn't make it work. I really couldn't turn it into income. Here is another lesson, don't quit. The profession works.

You just have to find the right vehicle, the right team, and the right timing. Don't compare to the people you see on stage. You hear the glory but don't know the story. Rocky didn't win in the ring, he won by punching frozen meat in the freezer, over and over again. Muhammad Ali said he hated every morning workout, but he loved being The Champ.

Focus on the end goal, and go for it. To get from where you are to where you want to be, follow this very simple 5 step formula

1 Figure out what you want

2 Find out who has what you want

3 Find out what they did

4 Do what they did

5 Don't quit

This is not an easy business. Life isn't fair. Business isn't fair. Network Marketing isn't fair. Eric Worre from GoPro is famous for saying Network Marketing isn't perfect, it's just better. Ray Higdon from RankMakers says make them an offer, give them an option to say no, and move on. Todd Falcone teaches how to prospect real estate agents. I learned from him to call RE agents from their for sale signs. "I saw your sign by the house on Main Street. I'm an entrepreneur working with an international marketing company. We work with a lot of RE agents locally and nationally. How long have you been in RE? Gandhi says "Be the change you want to see in the world." I say "be the change you want to see in the Network Marketing profession. One of my mentors taught me the concept of binoculars and blinders. Focus on your goals with binoculars, and keep on the blinders.

As you use binoculars to focus on your goals in life and in Network Marketing, imagine a 3 lane highway. If you are in the right lane, you are going slow. You see all the exit signs and they are all distractions. As you pursue your goals, all distractions are equal. You coast over into the middle lane. Now you are going at a pretty decent clip. You see some the exit signs, but you are focused and pass most of them by. You're passing by some people and some people are passing you. You drift into the left lane. You're now in fifth gear. You are going pretty fast. You are prospecting and recruiting. You are developing some customers. You are making some money. You then see another lane. All the way to the left. Cars full of people. You drift into the HOV lane - High Occupancy Vehicles. You are creating a team, providing customer service and building and training leaders. You are getting paid and you are helping your people get paid. Help your people have a good product experience, help them earn money, and they will be with you for a long. long time.

Go for it! Become a rockstar! Become a Network Marketing RockStar. You can do it. You can have it all. You. Can. Have. It. All.

See you at the next company event or at one of our million dollar masterminds.

To your success

Drew

www.drewberman.com

Bonus Chapter by Chris Salem

MASTER YOUR INNER CHAMPION – UNBLOCK EMOTIONAL BARRIERS TO HAVE SUSTAINABLE SUCCESS AT THE NEXT LEVEL

Chris Salem is a highly authentic person who for over four years has had a special passion for empowering and serving business leaders, entrepreneurs in various industries, sales executives, coaches, authors, speakers, and others, taking their business and life to another level. For many years, Chris has seen people aspiring to make changes and grow but struggled at different phases of their career and life. He is just like you, a regular person that has faced similar struggles. Chris shares from experience what has worked successfully through hard work and dedication to help in your challenges.

Over 20 years ago I was working relentlessly building wealth but emotionally, spiritually, and physically was bankrupt. This was tied to an unresolved root cause with my father associated with anger from my childhood. It nearly killed me twice with habits and behaviors that were destroying me while the whole time it appeared to others I was a true success by the wealth accumulated. In reality, the money meant nothing if my emotional, physical, and spiritual well-being were not synchronized. It took hitting tock bottom 19 years ago to have that "aha" moment to finally realize the solution to my problem starts with looking within you taking my moral inventory and learning to be in the moment for clarity. It took a good two years from that time to come full circle with my true self. I was able to experience true success living in the solution by resolving the root cause and having balance.

What is balance? It is being true to your purpose and not being distracted by shiny objects, surrounding yourself with family and love ones, nurturing your spirituality, maintaining healthy balance of emotional and physical health, and being present in the moment. Since completing this process back then I have created awareness about unblocking emotional barriers to have sustainable success at the next level through speaking engagements to organizations by working with business leaders, entrepreneurs, and all types of people as a Change Strategist and Wellness Advocate.

Have you asked yourself from time to time why your life has not unfolded the way you have envisioned! What holds you back from getting things accomplished and being successful? The answer lies with past events in childhood through the teen years which is the Cause that leads to Effects that most people live in that keep them trapped in self-doubt that leads to procrastination. Your habits and behaviors unconsciously in adulthood are tied back to trigger events that have molded you into a pattern of self-doubt or success. It is your inner critic that has a choice of tapping into the positive or negative that dictates your habits and behaviors that either server you or not long term.

For example, you see a man who has never been able to live up to his full potential with his career. He may have had a father that was overbearing and always on him to improve his performance or skills. He may have also felt neglected as his father was never there for important events or did not acknowledge him for his successes growing up. These are trigger events that develop the Cause that leads to the Effects that in adulthood will mold habits and behaviors that may be detrimental to his success due to self-doubt. Living in the effect will not change his current situation operating from self-doubt. The inner critic defaults to the negative and feeds of the Cause unconsciously that creates habits and behaviors that do not serve him. He has lived his entire life not being his authentic-self always looking to be someone else his dad or what other authoritative figures wanted him to be in life.

Another example is a man who struggles being overweight and cannot seem to gain respect from women in his life. He relatively had a decent upbringing with no traumatic events. However, his mother slightly domineering would often comment during his growing years to eat everything on his plate because good food is expensive and others in third world countries were not as fortunate as him. His mother while not malicious with intent planted a seed of guilt in this man as a boy. In addition to struggling being overweight without long term success despite using several weight release programs he also gravitated to women more dominant than him. See the pattern here. He was not conscious to this during his adult years and during coaching did not recognize this as first. It was only through consistent questions were we able to lock in this was his Cause. Once he acknowledged this as his Cause and truly forgave his mother and most important himself then fully release it was he able in time to adopt healthier habits. These new healthier habits and mindset allowed him to make better choices with food to keep the weight off and choose wisely with a woman that was not dominant and also not submissive.

Can someone that is stuck in life change and move toward success operating from a place of peace without anxiety? The answer is YES but only when you start with addressing the Cause(s) not the Effects in your life. Your life is an evolving story and can change when you choose to change for the better. Your life is not confined by past events that negatively affected you as they can used to only strengthen to what you can become in a positive way. The start to eliminate self-doubt begins with addressing the Cause(s). Go back and write down what they are even you perceive them not to really bother you. Often, people do not realize that certain events that happened long ago have affected their lives and play out every day in what they do that does not serve them. Confront the Cause by looking at yourself in the mirror. Accept responsibility and appreciate this negative experience if you created it. Acknowledge the cause if you did not create it but were of victim of this circumstance. Forgive the people that hurt you. You do not have to forget but just forgive. Let is go either way as the story of your life is always evolving and is not defined by just these Causes from trigger events. This can be scary for many people but the only way to release the Cause that creates the Effects that no longer serve you. You can also do with a therapist, coach, or trusted friend. Use them to build your strength in a positive way and continue to develop a story that operates from a place of joy, happiness, and peace rather than negative emotions such as anger, shame, and guilt.

When you release the Cause(s) and truly let go it will unlock the feeling of true peace and joy. You will know your life is about choices and when you come from your authentic self your story will only lead you to success over time. Coming from joy and peace your decisions to act promptly rather than procrastinate will be easier and the fear of failure less. You will have more confidence in your abilities coming from authentic-self and know the universe will play it part if you play yours with 100% commitment and action. You will know fear is just fear itself not tied to actual objective or goal you have planned. Know success is a journey not a destination and the only true failure in life are not to start, confront, or follow through to something you fear. Always know that fear is an illusion. It is not real but only appears so when you focus and give energy to it.

Fear can manifest itself in many forms and often stems from your current emotional state. Anger is a manifestation of fear that is directed outwardly at someone else while guilt and shame are forms of fear directed inwardly at ourselves. These faces of fear can sometimes be difficult to see in our daily lives. Here is an example when you operate from fear.

For example, back in my twenties I once bought a car through a salesman that was referred by a friend of mine. My friend me told this salesman was having some personal financial issues but was a genuine good person that helped his friends. The reason I decided to buy from him was because I held my friend's recommendation in high regard and always liked to help out people that helped others without expectations. I figured if he earned a commission from me for helping purchase a car this would be a win-win situation.

I wrote a check of $1,000.00 to hold the car I selected and handed over photocopies of my driver's license including three recent month statements from my bank. That same night after dinner, it dawned on me that I have handed over confidential documents to him without a second thought – documents that a conman can make full use of. I've read of conmen who used another person's documents to apply for loans and then disappeared, leaving the unsuspecting victim to settle the loan with the bank.

When I thought about it, I realize that I do not really know this person at all other than being referred by my friend. Who knows what kind of a person he is. Perhaps he may be in such deep debts that he might be desperate enough to cheat.

My train of thoughts just continues to move on from one fear to another, each thought making the fear bigger and more terrible than the one before. By the time I realize what I was doing to myself, I was about ready to panic. As it turns out, none of what I fear was true. This was an honest person just trying hard to earn a decent living. All the fear that was self-created serves only to perpetuate this negative habit.

Most of our fear arises in the same way - subtle and unsuspecting. It starts with one fearful thought, which leads to another and another. Before you know it, it has taken on a life of its own. If we are not careful or have very poor self-awareness, this type of habit can literally create panic in us.

This fear tendency is actually very common and we can see it in ourselves almost every day. When we are not aware of it, this tendency tends to perpetuate itself each time we allow it to manifest in us. The good news is that we can change this tendency simply by increasing our self-awareness through mindfulness. The sooner we see this pattern, the easier it is to stop it or replace it with something more positive. When we do this repeatedly, we eventually release the power that fear has over us.

The key is to focus the energy toward your goal, dream, or something you desire and not waste it on fear that truly in reality does not exist. It is a choice like anything in life. Growth and fulfilling your dreams only comes when you operate out of your comfort zone and do things that you initially fear. You can begin to change your life living for your "Why" and knowing fear is just a loss of your oneness with your true essence. Here are ten steps to minimize self-doubt.

10 Steps to Eliminate, Reduce, or Minimize Self Doubt to Achieve Success

1. Address and confront the Cause(s) that lead to the Effects that create self-doubt and to truly let them go through forgiveness.

2. Make the conscious choice to change toward success by looking at it as a journey and growth process not a destination.

3. Incorporate a daily schedule of meditation, personal development, clean eating, and exercise to create balance and overall well-being. Important life decisions are best made when grounded and coming

from a sense of peace, joy, happiness, and feeling of confidence.

4. Always be grateful where you are now and where you are going forward.

5. Be in the present moment always and know fear manifests itself when you dwell too much on the past and project too much into the future.

6. Come out of your comfort zone early and be willing to be consistent but never strive for perfection when it comes to adopting new habits that best serve you toward the journey of success. Never become complacent as greatest growth comes from outside your comfort zone.

7. Write down short term and long term goals and set up for attainable goals over time. Reward yourself in a positive way for each goal met along the way.

8. Recognize your fear and know it is fear itself and never label it as a feeling of nervousness or anxiety.

9. Always know failure is only when you do not start or follow through. If something does not work during this journey always look at it as a learning experience and part of the process to something better. The universe will test you and when you make the choice to really go for it through belief and action then the universe will untimely do its part.

10. Know and commit to action consistently with your "Why". Know your strengths and weaknesses. However, always focus on your strengths to be better not perfect and leverage your weaknesses to those that can address for you.

We are all worthy of success. It is a choice and process that comes from an internal place of peace and joy inside of you. The choice to listen to your inner critic will be either positive or negative. You will find success when you truly let go of the Cause(s) that create the negative effects that hold you back. Adopt healthier habits over time through the steps depicted above so more positive energy and greater motivation can lead you toward a better life. The choice again starts with you.

Chris Salem

www.chrissalem.com

Bonus Chapter by Jenna Knudsen

A WOMAN'S PERSPECTIVE

"There are two types of people in the world~ network marketers and everyone else." Someone said that to me about 10 years ago and my response was, "What's a Networker Marketer?"

Now what seems like a lifetime later, that comment still brings a smile to my face.

Let me share a crazy, adventurous story...the last decade of my life.

I'll back up a tiny bit further to set the stage for what was to unfold. Twelve years ago, I made the monumental decision to get divorced. My daughter, Katie Sky, was six years old and my son, Liam, was four. It was a decision that launched my life in a direction I could have NEVER imagined at the time.

52% of you know what I'm talking about when I say that divorce is challenging. Mine was especially difficult. I lost my horse farm, my home, my Volvo, my identity and truly~ my mind. I had the freedom that I wanted, but along with it came financial devastation and dark days of desperation. I was lost and drowning in sorrow and debt.

My life raft showed up unexpectedly. After dropping off my kids at school one day, a friend invited me to a "girls party" at her house the following weekend. I was excited and eager to be around women whose lives were not falling apart. I yearned for fun and a sense that life would be ok again. Someday. Somehow.

I got a babysitter, even though my budget could not afford it, and set off to have some much-needed girl time. It was endless fun, something that had been missing in my life for some time as it's hard to be sad and happy at the same time. A great benefit was I also got to meet some amazing women. One woman in particular just lit up the room and I was like a moth to light. As we were parting for the evening, she said, "You know, with everything that's happened in your life, I have something that may just turn things around for you. And then she invited me to be her guest and hear a local doctor speak about customized nutrition, improved health, and it also was a possible financial opportunity. She simply said: It's at his office this Thursday, want to join me?"

As her warm smile beamed at me, every cell in my body screamed, "YES! Yes, indeed I do!"

Did I have any idea what she was talking about?

Did I ask questions?

Did I give a hoot?

Absolutely not. I was just thrilled to be around energetic, positive women and gleeful over someone inviting me to another event. I had to create a new life for myself and these women seemed smart, fun, and in the know.

That Thursday found me at the office of a local podiatrist, a pillar in our community, amazing speaker and charming man- I was mesmerized. He shared about his life- his practice, running marathons and what living a healthy lifestyle meant to him. His energy was palpable. His words offered promise, hope and possibility. I hung on to every word, yet had no idea what he was offering.

At the end of the meeting, he came right over to me, looked straight into my eyes and asked, "So, will you be joining us?"

Joining? Wait, what??

I obviously was missing something.

"Joining?" I asked, with eyes wide, feeling slow.

"Yes, our team. This is a team business. Our company is a Network Marketing company. Are you joining us?" He spoke softly with a huge and friendly smile.

His warmth, the stories from others in the room and seeing successful, local business people had me feeling like something special was happening here. I felt energized and saw a group of supportive people that seemed like they wanted to help me.

I felt something good happening, but I just didn't get what.

This was my introduction to Network Marketing.

Then my new friend, the woman who invited me handed me a sign-up form. I got really nervous and was not sure what to do. Most times I would have said no and made up an excuse, " I can't afford it", or "I have to think about it". But not this night. Something inside me said, "Just do it". And I did.

I joined a Network Marketing company. I had no idea that's what it was. Those words were never officially said at the meeting. But I was now a Network Marketer! I joined because the people all seemed so smart and passionate. The products sounded amazing and they said there was money to be made. I needed to make money- end of story. I had lost so much- my farm, my car...I needed to rebuild our life.

I got home excited and called my Mother with the exciting news that I had "started my own business!" She asked lots of questions as moms do and I gave as many details as I could. At some point I muttered something about it being "Network Marketing."

"Wait, what did you say?" she asked.

"Oh, it's a type of business called Network Marketing." I replied.

"Honey. HONEY! What? You have a college education. Why would you do that? Isn't it illegal?" Isn't that one of those pyramid schemes? I heard her breathe heavily. Not a good sign.

"No Mom. It's not illegal. It's a business model that allows you to have your own business and earn as much as you want and, and, and..."

I found myself babbling, defending and making answers up because I could FEEL her doubting me through the phone.

"Listen Mom- a DOCTOR in my community is doing this, and a lawyer, and a dentist and lots of other smart business people...if it's good enough for them, then it's good enough for me." I was faking my confidence and wasn't even sure if I believed what I was saying, but I had already maxed out my credit card for the business starter kit and like hell was not going to stop now. I felt scared and excited at the same time. But for the first time since my divorce I also felt hope.

I hung up the phone and sighed. Oh God, PLEASE let Network Marketing be legit. And more importantly, please let this work for me because I need this so badly.

So that's how it all started. My first day in Network Marketing. I was "in". Yet I had no idea what I was into, nor what was in store for me. Now, 12 years later I can look back and know it was the positive energy of the people in that room that got me to say yes and start my business. Those people and many others have always helped me stay moving in the right direction.

So there I was, a newbie Network Marketer. Soon this giant box arrived in the mail with my Business Starter Kits. Now the realization hit hard. I'm "in" and I've bought the goods, I knew right away to pay off my credit card I had to sell them quickly or I would be further in debt. I decided to go for it. I drank the Kool-Aid. My motto was "Go big or go home"- this is my ticket out of doom and gloom and my pathway to a new life.

I attended every meeting and training. I bought books on Network Marketing. I went to company events where the energy was so high and the people were so happy, the only thing I can think is "What the HELL are these people ON?!" My next thought being, "And where can I get some??"

It seemed unreal. All this talk about "Personal growth", "Possibility" and "Living your best life!" People jumping up and down on stage, thousands of people cheering...it felt more like a U2 concert than a business event! This was my new culture. Excitement, no limits, shoot for the stars.

This is a good spot to pause and let you know Network Marketing *is* more like a U2 Concert than a business. Keep that in mind as you read this book! Making money, helping people and being successful CAN be fun!

OK, so back to the story at hand...I'm single, Mom of two toddlers and in need to make money to feed my kids and pay my rent. I show up for my team trainings with an open mind, a notebook and my favorite purple pen. I'm a note taker and I take furious notes.

What I learn is NOT what I thought I'd be learning. It wasn't about the science of our health products or the company...all that was online, taken care of by the company. What I was being taught was about life. Life skills. Personal growth.

I was trained to dig deep, peel back the layers of my soul and ask hard questions to find out WHAT DID I REALLY WANT in my life? And you know what they had the nerve to tell me? That I could do be and have anything I wanted in life! Can you imagine? The nerve! Telling a broke, single Mom that she had the right to live her dreams! That anything I wanted could be mine? Seriously? And then, the cherry on top... they would HELP ME get there.

I thought these people were off their rocker. Was this a new culture or just a cult? Damn it- could my Mom be right again?

Nope, she wasn't. But those were my initial thoughts. Never in my life had people cared so deeply about my dreams, my goals and how I wanted to live my life. So many people truly cared about me and they were all willing to step up and help me achieve it. It felt strange and weird, but it also felt like I was exactly in the right place for me.

I used every health product my company made and quickly became a product of the product. I was walking the talk and looked and felt amazing. People asked me what I was doing. I told them. They started using the products. They joined me. My team was building. My check grew. I kept sharing and teaching others. It was fun! It felt great! And my checks were putting food on my family's table, paying our rent and I was earning a living without having to go to a 9 to 5. I was able to be a mom to my young children at a time when they needed me most.

A year into my new business I felt as if I was living on a cloud, loving my daily routine and my budding business. Sharing healthy products that worked and made a difference in people's lives was a wonderful reward. Most satisfying to me was totally engaging with my new partners to help inspire them on what they want and to shift to being ok with wanting more. I loved helping them to make a plan. I loved to motivate and coach people to lead their best life. To dream again. Life was beautiful.

Just eighteen months into my new "business" something mind blowing happened. I walked out to the mailbox to get my check. I opened it on the country road I lived on. I thought my eyes were deceiving me. There were five figures on my check… before the decimal points. It was five figures! Over ten thousand dollars. One check. Ten grand. I stood there and cried.

What I didn't tell you was that after my divorce I had to file for bankruptcy. And did I mention my car was repossessed in the middle of the night? That was some morning waking up to my car missing and my children crying because there was no way to get them to school. Good times…not.

From bankruptcy and my car being repossessed, to seeing a check for over $10,000.00 seemed like a miracle from the angels. I remember that day thinking I had found the business of my dreams and, "I'll never do anything but Network Marketing." I was officially on fire and a true believer.

Now, let me be clear. I had SO many haters the entire time I was building my team. "This is a pyramid." "This is a scam." "Oh honey, are you still wasting your time with that "thing." And this was from my FAMILY. Friends were just as negative and I was continually finding myself defending what I was doing and why.

Even when the company paid for my brand-new BMW and my kids went to private school and I moved to a new house…they still poo-pooed my business." It's tough swimming upstream, let me tell ya. But hey, haters gonna hate. For me, I just kept on sharing, teaching and creating more success. I was fueled to be even more successful.

What I discovered eventually was that the more I moved away from the negative energy and the nay-sayers, the happier I became. I started hanging out with a new crowd. Positive people, positive energy. Believers in magic and miracles. Practitioners of a healthy lifestyle. People who really wanted to LIVE and GROW and LEARN. Smart business people who wanted to contribute and make a difference in other people's' lives. The haters, doubters and negative Nellies started to fade away. It just happened naturally and it felt liberating.

Four years in and I hit my stride! A huge team! Mailbox money every month. Traveling the country, sharing what we do! I was living the dream!

And then… (insert horror movie music...)

Our company owners announced that a HUGELY successful business person was partnering with our company and that would make us unstoppable. Checks would grow 10x. We would all be wonderfully wealthy. This tycoon was taking us global! He was going to use our company to show the world how professional and profitable Network Marketing could be! We'd be the new gold standard by which every other company would be measured! This was IT!! We had arrived! This was going to be THE BIGGEST THING EVER!!!

And then Thud. I'll spare you the gory and depressing details, but know this...it all went south. In a big way. I went from making a six-figure income to not getting paid ever again. No more checks. In the course of one year our company went from "We're going International" to "The doors are closing."

My life went sideways. Again. I couldn't even believe it. Everything I told people would NEVER happen to our company- was happening. Every negative thing that people had tormented me about over the years came true. Once again I was living a nightmare.

We lost our house. Again. I lost my car. Again. I lost my confidence. Again.

Here's what I didn't lose. All of the personal growth skills and knowledge that was driven into my brain over the past five years. All of the skills I'd acquired in coaching people to success. All of the digging deep into my soul to determine what I wanted out of life. The books, the courses, the mentors had embedded a success chip into my mind. Personal growth is just that. I had grown in so many ways. More than money could buy. I had what it takes to do anything.

My dreams were temporarily crushed, the business was closed, but my mind was open for anything. I was a different person now. I knew how to overcome obstacles.

Network Marketing brought so much to me.

My path- coaching.

My passion- getting back in the saddle and igniting my passion for horses.

My chosen family- my life partner and many of my best friends.

An ongoing thirst for personal growth and a desire to always be learning, seeking and becoming a better version of myself.

About this time I meet a dynamic man. His name is Drew Berman and he is a friend of a friend. He has a bright smile and a great laugh. He knew that my company had shut their doors (or more slammed it on our fingers!) and he gently approached me about joining HIS team with a different health company. I could not say "NO THANKS!" fast enough. He seemed great and I could tell he was successful, but getting back into Network Marketing was the last thing I wanted to do at that moment in time.

I needed a break to find myself and what I wanted to do now. What was my next step. Where did I want to invest my time. There was a part of me that said "no mas" Network Marketing.

Life goes on and kids have to eat and growing feet need new sneakers. So I did what I had to do in the moment. I got a job. A steady, safe job that kept food on the table. Unfortunately after all the personal freedom the J-O-B also began to suck the life out of me each day. I wanted to set my cubicle on fire. I had dreams of doing just that. But for a period of time, I reported to my cubicle every day and worked. The walls of my cubicle started to move in closer, day by day. The fluorescent lights burned my eyes and my very soul. I started praying for the weekend on Monday at 9am. I felt like crying every day.

I was so torn. One side of me knew that I had to be "responsible" and "adult" in a way that would pay the bills for myself and my children. Another side of me wanted to create, to be my own boss, live my life on my terms. My way. I could even hear Frank Sinatra ringing in my ears.

I survived the J-O-B for a year. And all during that time, Drew would check in with me on FB, like and comment on my blah posts, send me encouraging texts...never too much. Just a little bit of light in my dark day. He was just "there" ` reminding me of the light that I used to bask in with my old company. He was consistent, a positive energy and always left me feeling better about myself and life when we communicated. He did not pester me about "joining him" in his business, he simply was a friend. That left a huge impression on me.

I started writing in a journal~ using it more like a planner. I started fresh again. I wrote out what I wanted now to be in my life. What my "ideal" day would look like. What I liked doing and why. What made me truly happy. What made me most miserable.

I asked for "my path" to be shown to me. Every day I asked. And then one day it came... Women were asking me to coach them. They loved how I helped them when we were building a team together. They too wanted more and they asked for my help. To coach them. Coach them? Hmmmm....this sounded interesting.

Personal growth had become a huge passion for me. Ever since my life spun out of control, I was more interested than ever in ways to turn it around and head in a direction best for me. Before personal growth entered my life I was all about following the path society said I should follow. Personal growth showed me I could follow my own path. We only get to go around once in life. We should be doing what makes us happy and what inspires us.

Finding my own mentor, writing, journaling and planning had all become daily habits of mine that were transforming my life. I had coached hundreds of people to success as part of my Network Marketing team... why not solo?? And so my career as Jenna Knudsen, Fun Coach began! This was now calling to me. It energized me again.

My first coaching clients were people from networking marketing companies who wanted success and wanted to go to the next level. It was fantastic. We developed mindset shifts and challenges, created daily success systems, practiced planning and created accountability. Their personal businesses and checks soared.

I was thrilled to coach many to success from different Network Marketing companies. I was also asked to join all of them. I said no to all, even the ones with the special deals. I loved coaching. I also felt some personal PTSD. And how could I could pick just one? Not possible.

One of my successful coaching clients sent a gratitude gift to me. A "thank you" package arrived at my doorstep and I thought, 'Well, I can't let it go to waste. It is a thank you gift after all." She had no expectation, she was seriously jazzed that we had crushed her goal!

So, with no expectation, but full of appreciation, I started using the health system. Fast forward a month...I had lost 14lbs of stubborn belly fat and my muffin top was no longer popping out over my breeches! My energy was through the roof, I was sleeping like a baby and my sense of well-being was at an all-time high. Crazy great results! Huh, who knew?

Well, I knew now that I loved these products as much as I had loved my prior company's products. And as fate would have it, Drew Berman called me (totally unaware that I was using products from his company with great success)....and asked me if I was open to flying out to Arizona to meet the owners of his company. He got Kathy Coover on the phone and we chatted for 30 minutes and she was an instant girlfriend. Open, upbeat, real and completely amazing energy...this woman lit me up like the Christmas tree in Rockefeller Center! Her energy was contagious and before I knew what was happening Doug & myself were flying out to Arizona to check out a company, products and a lifestyle.

Drew met us in Arizona and we discovered an amazing company, founders with vision, passion, perseverance and integrity & fabulous products that changed lives. In Drew we found someone who was devoted, passionate and truly in this for all of the best reasons.

Everything I was fearful of was tossed and my excitement and passion to create a successful business around healthy products was ignited once again. This time it was woven in alongside my passion for coaching, so I would have two streams of income. It's a brave new world in entrepreneurship and you can truly create success in limitless ways! One of Drew's strongest traits is meeting people where they're at and creating success from that point. And that's what we did.

Today I am an Equestrian Lifestyle & Mindset coach. I've created a career around my greatest passions~ horses, health and living a life you love! I have coaching clients & an equestrian community from around the world, known as "Smarties." Our community is all about ' Equestrians empowering equestrians." I'm the creator of the first daily planner designed exclusively for Equestrians called "The S.M.A.R.T. Equestrian Planner." In this planner you are guided to create vision pages, establish goals, practice daily intention setting and gratitude, and prioritize your days.

This leads to happier, more productive days. More creation, less stress. I teach and coach habits, rituals and accountability. This is all embedded into the daily planner so that planning become the new norm. Success comes from sustainability. I'm coaching for everyone's long-term success!

Much of what I have learned and now teach are the same principles that moved me from anxiety and depression to calmness, confidence, and success. And all was learned from doing. And for that I have to thank Network Marketing for entering my life.

My life now centers around the equestrian lifestyle. Riding, horses and the equestrian life require major energy, strength and mental clarity. All of this is possible through products that support your health. Horses and riding are also quite an expensive passion, so residual income comes in quite handy.

Drew loves that I've found my niche in the Network Marketing world and outside of it as well. He supports me and my organization in every way possible. It's such a win/win/win...this is what's beautiful about our industry....everything is possible.

My last twelve years have been an incredible journey that started from a simple meeting. It has transformed from a desperate and bankrupt single Mom to a successful businesswoman and coach. I have my own Equestrian business alongside a powerful health brand...it's been an amazing, magical and powerful journey! I credit so much of this to the incredible power of what the Network Marketing profession teaches and also the outstanding leaders it attracts!

The raw truth...Network Marketing is NOT for everyone. It's for people who believe in the magic and power of their dreams. It takes courage, perseverance and devotion. It takes being a team player and truly caring about the success of others. It takes a love of personal growth and inner soul-searching. It takes having a courageous spirit. It takes kicking your comfort zone to the curb! It takes failing 9 times and getting up 10! It takes ignoring haters and dream stealers while smiling in the face of doubters and not asking anyone's permission to live the life you're currently dreaming of. It takes every ounce of grit you got, but oh hell is it worth it!

So, yes, it is a choice...you choose to be a Network Marketing professional or you choose not to be.

When Network Marketing appeared in my life I said yes...I traveled this road and that has made all the difference!

Big love to all of my seekers of fun, freedom and financial abundance.

I created a life I love… and so can you.

Big love,

Jenna

Equestrian Lifestyle & Mindset coach.

www.jennaknudsen.com

Bonus Chapter by Philip Sasso

FROM BROKE MUSICIAN TO NETWORK MARKETING PROFESSIONAL

A man who is a partner, mentor and friend is Philip Sasso. He is actually part of my upline support team. We tend to not say upline and downline, we say support team and success team. Philip has been in 18 companies so he has seen the good the bad and the ugly of this wild profession over the last 30 years. He has earned 5 figures in a month, 6 figures in a year and 7 figures in a career. Philip has a heart of gold, and knows products, people, and comp plans. I am glad I have the opportunity to work with him. Enjoy.

I remember that day well! I was being introduced to Network Marketing and feeling a sense of hope and excitement, something that I hadn't felt in a long time. After studying music at college, and having played music in original rock bands in New York City, Los Angeles and a stint in Korea, I also taught guitar privately, bartended, did odd jobs and had a house painting business. All done, of course, so I could support myself while in pursuit of a career in music for which I had trained and studied...

On the day I was introduced to this new (to me) concept known as "Network Marketing," I was working at a telemarketing firm in Bellevue Washington. I found it to be one of the most depressing times in my adult life. The job was monotonous, and I was surrounded by people who were generally miserable. My co-worker, Sally, had come into the office that day all excited and animated. I asked her to tell me what was going on in her life that was so good, and she fairly bubbled over with her good news. "I've found an awesome business, and finally I'm gonna be able to have a good income and have time freedom." I immediately found myself drawn into her excitement as she explained to me that she had met a doctor and that this doctor would be able to tell me all about it. I was curious, and so when Sally got me on the phone with her, we made an appointment to meet at a hotel restaurant. I had never heard of a business like this before, but it sounded like a great concept. I was very interested. However, I didn't have the money to get started with this particular company, but I was determined to become involved as an associate, so I pawned one of my guitars to get the start-up money for it. That turned out to be one of the best decisions I've ever made. Participating in this business immediately surrounded me with people who were thinking bigger in life and typically maintained a very positive attitude. Early on I was to meet someone in the business who was actually making what I would've considered an *annual* income...but making this amount *per month*! It was eye-opening.

Over time among the things I came to love about this business was the fact that I had not needed to go to school for training and education to learn how to do it. My experience was that I was getting plenty of support. I could earn while I learned, and that was awesome. My start-up costs had been pretty low. (Thank goodness, because I had already racked up four years of college tuition debt and loan payments. I didn't need more of that!)

It has been so satisfying to realize that there are practically no limits on who I can speak to about this business; in fact, it is easy to invite anybody, regardless of their education level, gender, ethnicity or age (as long as they are over 18) to join with me. There are so many people, who, needing more income, realize the possibilities that come with a business like this. There are no limits or inequalities in payments; e.g., there is no "glass ceiling." This is an equal pay industry, unlike the normal job world where men usually get paid more. In fact, women do very well in Network Marketing, and I have been happy to have had the opportunity to introduce this business to women who have turned their lives around financially. Interestingly, early on I came to realize that anyone would want to be in a company that appeals to women, when they find out that in our industry for every successful man, there are three successful women. Women "get it" and they have been very influential in making us great!"

I'm always astounded at the fact that we literally can build a residual income where we are able to make money, even while sleeping. (It's happening!) I have come to realize that the only way one can have true time freedom in one's life is to have a residual income. Otherwise, it's just "trading hours for dollars." My actual realization of this fact: I have been able to reside anywhere I have desired, and thus in Network Marketing I have never been compelled to live where my "job" was located. This is not a "job." I am independently able to expand my business anywhere I choose to live, and anywhere I am at any given time...

After participating in different Network Marketing companies, I was fortunate to be introduced to the company I am with at this time. I have been with it from its "day one." However, my participation in many years of Network Marketing as a business has helped me gain insight into what to look for in a good company. What are the factors that make for a good company? Very importantly, there are many different compensation plans out there, and I found many of them were very difficult for the average person to achieve any success with. Of all the plans I participated in, my favorite is the binary compensation plan. Among the features I like about this plan, is that you only have to build two teams... and you are able to place new associates underneath other established associates in your team as they come into the business. This creates a synergistic effect, i.e., more of a community, which can be mutually helpful. I did not find previous plans offering this when I did multi-level marketing or plans that were called "stair-step breakaways" or breakaway plans. In those plans you were taught to build "wide" and one had to have many teams in order to have a great income. The saying in those types of this industry is that you (need to make sure you) build width for wealth... as well as depth for longevity; *whereas,* in a binary plan, such as the one I participate in, you are doing that *simultaneously.* In my opinion, the binary plan is brilliant compensation to the next level. I have found that there are different "binary" plans, but all were not created equal. However, I must say that I always had more success with those companies that did have any kind of a binary plan. I was very happy to find that the company I am with now has, in my opinion, the best binary plan, coupled with products that are truly helping people with their health and wellness. In fact, I look at it this way: What good is making a lot of money if you don't have great health? So if you have a company that provides the best product line for the best health support, coupled with the best opportunity to have substantial wealth, you've got a grand slam.

Being a baby boomer, I realize how important it is to maintain my health and have a plan for my financial future. Many baby boomers, of which there are 72 million of in the United States, do not have much savings and are in poor health. Having been with many different companies on my path to finding the right one, I realize it has also been very fortunate that my company's management team really knew what they were doing when setting it up, including that it has always had substantial financial backing. It's important to me that the company has a culture wherein people help each other. I also realized how important it is to constantly pursue personal development in one's own life, and it is gratifying to see a company embrace those principles and teach them to their associates. In my experience I have also found that many companies in this industry get very stale. I look for a company that is very innovative and keeps up with the times. I want a company that does not charge a monthly fee for the website that you are using for your own business. I am always amazed when I see a company charging $29 or $40 a month for a website. I want a company where when you purchase their product you are getting real value for your purchase. I want to see a program that will not cost money above and beyond the cost of one's food budget. I do not like companies that charge people $300 or more and the company pays bonuses on that and the new associate gets nothing for that initial startup fee. They are told they have "a business". I look at these companies as a disguised money game. I prefer a company that is debt-free. And privately owned. It is very important that the company has consumable products that people will buy every month at a fair price. When it comes to a health and wellness company I want to see real studies that have been done on these products. Many companies make untrue assertions that they have conducted studies. These studies were usually done on individual ingredients and done outside of the company, and not even on their own company's product line!

I think it's important that the company I'm with is attractive to young people in addition to people who want to maintain health and wellness well into later life. These days, people in their 20's, who are now known as "millennials," do not want to work the 9-to-5 job as their parents did. Many of them have incredibly high student loan payments after college and are forced to move back home with their parents. They simply cannot afford to live on their own. Our industry gives them the opportunity to be able to have the time to enjoy their lives and the money to help pay for their student loans and have a place of their own. Many of them want to travel and this business can help them do just that.

I am very grateful and very proud to call myself a professional network marketer. It has given me the opportunity to have the six-figure income I now enjoy and the time freedom that comes with it. This profession creates more six and seven figures than all other industries combined. I believe the only people who are not associating themselves with this business are the ones who don't understand it. In fact, they comprise the majority of our population. This gives those who are involved with Network Marketing at this time an incredible opportunity to share this business model with that majority and, in turn, to help others do the same. The people who do well in this industry are people who don't make it "about themselves," but instead have made it about others. In fact, as it works out, the more people you help get what they want or need from doing this business, the more you will have, as well.

When I first met the doctor who showed me this business the one thing she said to me that I will never forget was this: "You will have ups and downs in this business but in the end it will be so worth it. Never, never, never quit!" I never did and she was right. It *has* been so worth it!

Philip Sasso

Executive Trainer

Action Steps

FREE GIFT!!

Now that we are done with the book, let's continue our relationship. I want you to have a free gift. Go to www.drewberman.com and get your free training on prospecting and recruiting.

It's the exact system I used to enroll

» A professional actor from another country and help him create a residual income for over a decade

» A woman who had been in over a dozen companies, found me online, then hired me to be her coach

» A 7 figure earner, Network Marketing Professional, no longer in love with his company, looking for his next chapter. This man was a Networker in transition

» A successful entrepreneur who was looking for a way out of his successful business so he can have more free time, and

» A young nurse who wanted more then anything a side income that would replace just one nursing shift so she can spend more time with her daughters.

Until we meet again

Love yourself and love others.

Be the change you want to see in the Network Marketing Profession.

Know that if you want to change your life, you have to change your life. Because if nothing changes, nothing changes.

Don't compare yourself to the people on stage.

Do the best you can. Don't beat yourself up.

Practice your presentation in the mirror. Often.

Celebrate all victories, even the minor ones.

Come visit me at www.drewberman.com - I got some cool stuff for ya.

Connect with me on social media, let's get to know each other.

I hope to see you at the next event and hear about your journey and your success. Let's meet up at a master mind, a summit or on the beaches of the world.

You got this.